DABBLING IN DALMATIA

Michael Fawcett

A Bright Pen Book

Text Copyright © Michael Fawcett 2010

Cover design by Jamie Day ©

All rights reserved. No part of this publication may be reproduced, stored in a retrieval system, or transmitted in any form or by any means, electronic, mechanical, photocopy, recording or otherwise, without prior written permission of the copyright owner. Nor can it be circulated in any form of binding or cover other than that in which it is published and without similar condition including this condition being imposed on a subsequent purchaser.

British Library Cataloguing Publication Data.
A catalogue record for this book is available from the British Library

ISBN 978-07552-1313-9

Authors OnLine Ltd
19 The Cinques
Gamlingay, Sandy
Bedfordshire SG19 3NU
England

This book is also available in e-book format, details of which are available at www.authorsonline.co.uk

To Robi and Erika

Introduction

One of the great debates facing many people in every generation as they approach retirement is: "What on earth are we going to do!!"
For some it is not a problem, as they intend to go on working, and good on them, but that was not for me nor my wife March; and certainly not working for other people. Many people have consuming hobbies or pastimes and intend to go on indulging in them in retirement. Some just want to relax, reflect on the past and wallow in not doing anything.
Our debate started well before retirement. We decided that firstly, we would take early retirement, at 60 or earlier. This was largely motivated by what was happening to friends and acquaintances, who were either dying off all around us, or contracting serious illnesses. We thought we would hopefully give ourselves more time to do whatever we decided upon.
Secondly, and in particular, we wanted some sort of adventure; something quite different.

Living in Jersey, which though a lovely place to live, is rather restrictive in its 45 square miles for some sort of adventurous life. We both had consuming hobbies; me oil painting and March machine embroidery. But we couldn't see ourselves spending the rest of our lives enjoying these pursuits, doing the same rounds of restaurants, walks, drives and summer holidays.

So, do we buy a yacht and sail around the world, or become ancient backpackers trekking the Himalayas, or perhaps go on adventurous holidays dog-sleighing in Alaska, or what?

We had certainly come to the conclusion that we would have to move abroad, but where? I had plenty of experience of moving around and living abroad in the years I spent in the army. However, March was Jersey born and had spent all her life there, except for the war years away from Jersey, but she too was looking for an adventure away from Jersey, or simply just to do something different in her retirement.

For some years we had been holidaying in France and had on many occasions looked over properties in the many regions we visited, with the thought that perhaps France would be the place to live. Certainly France is very different and a big and beautiful country with everything: sea, mountains, rivers, beautiful countryside and Paris. What is more learning French would be a challenge.

However, though we had fallen in love with many of the areas we visited, nothing seemed to meet our criteria, which were obviously too exacting. The houses were either too small or far too big with far too much land. Some were pretty dreadful – as though the cows had just been moved out. Many areas we ruled out because there were far too many Brits living there! For the same reason we ruled out Spain.

Many Jersey folk have second homes in Normandy or Brittany, but this was not what we were looking for; if it was to be France we would need to be down south, not just for the better climate but we could use it as a springboard for travels eastward, to Italy and beyond.

*

Then things took a slightly different turn. Two things happened pointing us in a different direction.

Firstly, we saw on television a holiday programme hosted by that lovely woman Jill Dando. This was broadcast just before she was murdered. She was in Croatia and in particular was describing the lovely little seaside resort of Bol on the Island of Brac; Bol is famous for its distinctive golden beach shaped like a toucan's beak. Also for its tennis tournaments. The little harbour was full of little wooden fishing boats and looked just like Greece. We were quite captivated by the programme which was so well presented by Jill. Would this be the sort of place we would retire to?

Secondly, I received a call from my son Mark in Croatia. He was working for the OSCE in Zagreb after spending some time in the "interior" after all the troubles. He announced that he met a Croatian girl working in the same HQ and they had planned to get married the following year. We were invited to fly out to meet her but due to various commitments I flew out as the Family's chief emissary to vet the fiancée!

After meeting his bride to be and phoning around the family with my approval, I was whisked off for a few days to explore Dalmatia from Split to Dubrovnik.

It was only two years since the bitter conflict in the Balkans had ended and the evidence of the war was there in abundance; many of the battles had taken place close to Zagreb and we were soon seeing burnt out houses riddled with bullet holes, followed by ethnically cleansed villages all the way to Split on the Adriatic coast.

My son had done two 6 month tours with the British Army during the war in Bosnia and later having left the Army had been an EU Monitor followed by a tour with OSCE. With his good command of the language he was therefore an excellent guide.

I took an immediate liking to Split with its ancient Roman centre, waterfront and harbour, and the magnificent views out to the islands and Dinaric Alps, which surrounded the city. The drive down the coast to Dubrovnik was stunning; reminiscent of the drive from Sorrento to Amalfi in Italy. There were steep sided mountains to our left and clear blue sea and numerous islands to our right.

We stayed in a little apartment in the outskirts of Dubrovnik and proceeded to explore the ancient city, which was still being repaired after the considerable damage inflicted by the Serbs in the Balkan war; there was plenty of evidence of the numerous artillery and tank shells which hit the city. In spite of all this, repairs were well in hand and it did not distract from the beauty of the place. I certainly fell in love with its Venetian architecture and its fascinating streets, the stone pavings so polished by peoples feet that the streets looked shiny and wet. Lunch was at a little restaurant in a little side street, we christened it "Mrs Migginses", because the proprietress looked very like Mrs Miggins in the Black Adder. The grilled small squid in garlic butter sealed my love of Dubrovnik. March must see Dalmatia I said to myself – this might be part of what we were looking for.

*

A year later March and I went out to Croatia to meet the new In-Laws following Mark's three weddings (well one wedding and two blessings); we had managed the first two in Prague and England but not the one in Bosnia-Herzegovina.

We took the same route from Zagreb to Split and followed that glorious coastline towards Dubrovnik before we turned off crossing the Dinaric Alps to Bosnia-Herzegovina. Whilst not being too impressed with the Croatian hinterland before Split, she was enthralled with Dalmatia and its coastline, blue sea and islands.

'This is really heavenly' she exclaimed. 'And different.'

Perhaps the germ of an idea for an adventure had

been planted. It would certainly warrant consideration and investigation.

What follows is how this idea developed into our adventure in Dalmatia

Chapter 1

Why Croatia?

In spite of a slight chill in the air it was a lovely sunny January afternoon as we drove onto the harbour wall in Split on the Dalmatian coast. Blue and white ferries of all shapes and sizes and mostly pretty ancient were busying themselves in and out of the harbour like bees around their hive. But alas, our ferry, the 2pm ferry to the Island of Brac (pronounced Brach) was just disappearing round the end of the breakwater and the next one was not until 4.30pm so we had some time to kill. We stretched our legs and enjoyed the harbour scenes and the view across to Brac and the other islands off Split. Whilst we watched, our little Highland Terrier Rupert busied himself in his usual way by peeing on everything he could cock his little legs to. I cursed myself as I realised that the second beer I had at our much-needed stop for a break on the road from Zagreb, had probably caused us to miss the ferry.

I was also disappointed that my wife March would not see the house we had bought on the Island in daylight.

Although I had seen it, it was just a photograph to her. We had bought it on a whim after a lovely holiday in Croatia the previous year after a friend had found it for us and I had later flown out on my own to clinch the deal. It was to be our holiday home in the sun.

We had sold our house in Jersey and put all our furniture and possessions into store with the intention of finding a home in France, but so far we hadn't found anything. Our little house on Brac therefore, was our only haven for the time being.

So there we were with our car looking a bit like an oversized turtle, with its roof box, and laden to the hilt with our immediate possessions. I began to wonder what we were doing in a country that we knew little about; beautiful though it was it was still part of the Balkans with all its troublesome and bloody history. What lay ahead of us I was thinking, and no doubt so was March. A slight feeling of trepidation was beginning to creep into my bones. For March's sake though I had to be happy and confident, which was something I had learned to do in the Army whenever things were not going well. A little 'bullshit' can often be quite useful. "Bullshit baffles brains" was often bandied about.

However, after a long drive from Austria where we had been skiing with our family over Christmas, it was pleasant to stroll in the winter sun. Split, an ancient Roman city, with Diocletian's palace and its Venetian architecture, looked lovely nestling below the Dinaric Alps, which towered above the city. Looking across the shimmering blue Adriatic sea at the Island, whilst we sat in a café on the quayside, I secretly wondered, were our doubting friends in Jersey right, that Croatia was still an uncivilised war zone.

*

"Why Croatia"? Our friends in Jersey were continually asking us.

Well, this was a valid question, as they knew that it was not what we had originally planned. We had for many years been looking in France for a permanent place to live. We felt that Jersey was losing its charm; the Island's economy becoming almost entirely based on its off shore finance industry. This required people to service the industry, so building grew at a pace and the roads had become full of cars; almost as bad as in a London rush hour. St Helier, was becoming unrecognisable from the charming town we knew. Whilst we still loved the Island, which was March's birthplace we were feeling a bit restricted.

Like many British people we had already become involved in the British love affair with France. Many Jersey people have holiday homes across the water in Brittany and Normandy but we were looking for warmer climes further south. Also, now that our children had all left home we were looking to travel more and perhaps to have a few 'adventures'. Jersey was no longer the best place to base ourselves. Before we became too old or infirm we had to find somewhere where we would have more freedom of movement; just getting into a car and driving to wherever would be quite different.

Our search to buy a property in France had been fraught with many disappointments. We had searched over the years in many regions and had seen many lovely properties but none had met our criteria. Often they were far too isolated or way beyond our budget. Most of the properties we were shown were almost derelict and looked as though the cows had just moved out. French estate agents also have a bad habit of wasting your time by taking you to properties, which did not meet any of the requirements we had laid down.

Then at last we found a really lovely house right on the River Dordogne. It was not one hundred percent what we wanted; it was not as big as we would have liked and it did not have additional outbuildings for turning into Gites to generate an income or to make a studio for my painting and March's fabric art. However, it was really pretty and was only a few feet from the river where we envisaged our ourselves, our children and grandchildren being able to swim, fish and canoe. Alas, our dreams were shattered when after we had made an offer, we were told that someone else had beaten us to it. Amazingly they had offered £7,000 less than our bid but had clinched the deal by offering the seller a months holiday every year for five years!!! We were obviously not going to be as lucky as the people we had read about in magazines who had seen the house of their dreams on their first look in the estate agent's window.

We decided that we would never find the right house in France unless we were living on the spot. So we decided to sell our house in Jersey and rent a property in France. However, as always in life events often take a quite different course from what you plan.

*

The link with Croatia was already established through our son Mark who worked for the OSCE in Zagreb and my visit to see him just after the war there. He had just married a Croatian girl whose parents live in Medjugorie in Herzegovina. In the summer of 1999 we decided to visit him and also take up an invitation from the in-laws to visit them in Medjugorie.

On our drive down there we were captivated by the beauty of the Dalmatian coast, with the clear blue Adriatic sea, the mountains along the coast and the many picturesque resorts and fishing villages. There were no signs that only a few years before there had been a terrible war raging in Croatia, Bosnia and Herzegovina.

After a pleasant stay with the in-laws, where we sampled the local cuisine, home made wine and slivovic, we had a few days to explore the Dalmatian coast. We decided to base ourselves in the coastal resort of Makarska, which with its Venetian architecture bedecked in borgonvilia and seafront cafes between the palm trees, looked very like resorts in Italy we had visited. We were already beginning to wonder whether there might be a seaside cottage to buy. However, unlike France where there are estate agents in every town and village, in Croatia there seemed to be none at all.

Remembering Jill Dando's programme we arranged to meet a developer cum property dealer on the large island of Brac, just off the coast near Makarska. On the Islands properties were supposedly cheaper than on the mainland. We caught the small car ferry from Makarska to the pretty fishing port of Sumartin on Brac and then drove the fifteen miles to the popular resort of Bol where we met Mr Zgelko. Tall, thin and topped with the strangest looking wig, Mr Zgelko was the archetypal estate agent cum property dealer. Speaking in glowing terms about the properties and apartments he had built or converted for wealthy Germans he also showed us a piece of isolated land high on a hill with a panoramic sea view where he said he could build us a house. His proud boast was that Bol was "the in place" with visiting film stars and international tennis players for the tournaments there. That was not our scene at all. He was not amused when we said that although Bol was a pretty resort it was too busy and touristy.

The second appointment we had on Brac was with a girl friend of Mark's secretary who came from Sumartin. Lucjia, or Lucy as she said we could call her, was like many Croatian girls, very tall, good looking, tanned and charming. Lucy lived with her retired parents on Brac after having to leave her job and apartment in Belgrade because of the war. She was teaching latin at the secondary school in Bol and spoke fluent English. She had a couple of places to show us but neither was of interest; one was a house in the trees with no view and the other was a dilapidated cottage on the harbour wall in Sumartin. After tea her father gave us a lovely stone clock he had made from the famous Brac stone which has also been used in the White House in the USA. This was our first experience of the amazing generosity of the Croatians and particularly those from Brac. We said our fond farewells and decided to drive around that end of the island before catching the ferry back.

We meandered along the surprisingly good roads lined with olive groves when suddenly we saw a sign pointing to Povlja, a small fishing village on the north coast. With still some time to kill we decided to have a look. As we approached the coast, still quite high up(the island is 872 meters at its highest), we saw the mountains on the mainland and the stretch of sea between and then suddenly below us the most picturesque harbour and village we had ever seen. Around every bend, as we descended the zig-zag road, the views of Povlja became even more impressive. Having taken up painting professionally in recent years I knew I just had to paint these scenes one day.

Povlja is a natural harbour with several inlets, the largest of which has harbour walls and houses on three sides. Many of the houses are in the old Venetian style, some with balconies, and roofed in either red pantiles or stone slabs on the older ones. The main part of the village rises up steeply to the church and old Roman fort; Povlia derives its name from the Roman name Paulia..

Around the harbour we noted four bars/cafes, a post office and a village shop. The harbour was packed with small fishing boats and some small pleasure boats. The quays were dotted with piles of fishing nets and children played happily. Hardly a car was to be seen. Sitting at an outside table in one of the cafes we both knew instinctively that this was the place for us.

Our stay was too short as we had to catch the last ferry back to Makarska but that night we phoned Lucy from our hotel and said that if she heard of any houses or apartments for sale, we would be very interested.

*

Back in Jersey, little did we know how fast things would move. Six weeks later we had a letter from Lucy giving details and photos of a house for sale at the 'Punta', the point at the entrance to the harbour. We decided that I should fly out as soon as possible to have a look.

Armed with camera and video camera I flew to Zagreb and from there in a small plane of Croatian Airways to the Island's small airport near Bol. Coming in to land I could see that the island was quite big; about 30 miles by 10 miles (about four times the size of Jersey) with a few scattered small villages in the interior and small fishing ports dotted around the coast. Rather like Greece, the Island was rocky and covered in scrub, small trees and olive groves. Lucy and her Father were there to meet me and take me to the hotel in Povlja where I was to stay the night before our appointment to view the house the next day. I was lucky to get a room in the hotel as it had been taken over by the British Army who used it as a water sports training centre, where soldiers on duty in Bosnia could spend a few days sailing, windsurfing, diving and other adventurous pursuits. The fact that my son had told them that I was an old ex regular soldier probably clinched the room.

The following morning I walked with Lucy and her Father out to the Punta, where a handful of stone houses had been built by the sea about twelve years ago, before the Balkan war. The owner, a Mr Zdinjvic from Imotski on the Bosnian border, was unable to be there so his friend from the village was there with the key.

The house, which was a stones throw from the sea, was stone faced and set in a sizeable walled garden covered in silvery grey plants and a strange succulent. A few small trees with feathery leaves were dotted about the garden with a fig tree and an olive tree. Into the house I marched with cameras working overtime. There were two good-sized bedrooms, a small bathroom, a living room and a kitchen through an archway. Opening the windows and shutters the house had lovely views but I was not prepared for the stunning view which confronted me as I threw open the French windows onto the sunny terrace. There before me was the clear blue Adriatic sea, the Island's coastline stretching away to the west towards Split and in front of me the five mile stretch of sea to the mainland, whose mountains swept down to the sea with little villages and resorts nestling at their feet. It was enchanting, but now I had to get back to Jersey to sell it to March.

It didn't take much selling even though I am pretty useless with any camera and particularly a video camera. The pictures had turned out well even though I had managed to leave the video camera switched on and filmed my feet during the five minute walk back to the village. March then noticed a photograph of the house behind. There was a sign saying Pizzeria – Grill.

"What's this?" she exclaimed. We then debated whether it was a good idea to live next to a Pizzeria with the potential of noise on a warm summer evening. In the end we felt that it might be a good point if we let the house when we weren't there. We need not have worried as the Pizzeria was to become a little haven for us during our forthcoming life in Povlja.

We then went ahead and offered to pay the asking price; we had already heard that Mr Zdinjvic was not prepared to negotiate. Our son found us a lawyer, a husband and wife team, in Makarska and I flew out again to complete the transaction accompanied by my son who spoke good Croatian. We met Mr Zdinjvic in the lawyer's office if you could call it that as it was not much larger than a kitchen cupboard and barely able to house the five of us.

Mr Zdinjvic, a schoolteacher from Imotski on the Bosnian border, could easily have passed for a bandit if he had tied a coloured scarf around his head. Solidly built, he had a red puffy face with a drooping moustache hanging over a wicked grin and had a handshake which took some time to recover from. He wore a rough hairy sports jacket, a purple shirt, red tie and a pair of baggy trousers. I could see that I wouldn't get anywhere if I tried to haggle over the price. Papers were duly signed and a visit made to the town hall to sign more papers. I agreed to arrange transfer of the deposit and the final payment by Christmas, which was only two months away.

This was when we could have taken possession. It was also the first year that foreigners had been able to buy property in Croatia for some time, but the purchase, although we had passed contract and our name entered into the 'Book of Land', would have to be rubber stamped by the Foreign Ministry in Zagreb. We were assured by the lawyers that this would be a formality, as none had been refused so far and my son was married to a Croatian after all.

Some time before this, the sale of our house in Jersey had gone through and all our furniture and possessions put into store. Still frustrated by our lack of success in finding a house in France that summer we were keen to start our adventure. Then, after much discussion on what we should do, I said:

"What if we went on from Christmas in Austria to take over our house in Croatia in January, 'do it up' for a few months and move on to France in the Spring to find a house?" March did not exactly fall over gushing with praise at my brainwave but after some consideration she agreed on the plan. At least we would be on our way.

We bought a 'Thule' to go on the roof of our estate car, both of which were crammed full of clothing and things we thought we would need; not forgetting our dog Rupert and all his paraphernalia.

When some of our friends heard we were really going off to live in Croatia they thought we were mad. Bruno, an Italian restauranteur friend in Jersey suggested that we take a gun with us! The reaction in general was that we were going to a war zone and a country full of barbaric people. We were unable to convince friends and relatives that Croatia was rid of the war, which had not touched much of the coast and had not touched our island at all. Their ears were also deaf to reassurances that the people were friendly and Dalmatia was beautiful and not torn by war.

Having said our fond farewells to friends and relatives who seemed to think that they would never see us again, we set off for Luxembourg, on route to Christmas in Austria, to see our son Richard who worked there. Luxembourg was in a festive mood with street fairs full of Christmas goodies, food stalls and small bars selling piping hot gluhwein and smart shops full of Christmas presents. Christmas in Austria was also a joyous festive occasion with some of our children and grandchildren. But soon we had to tear ourselves away and head for Croatia. The weather was bitterly cold and the roads icy as we crossed through Slovenia, which has much the same scenery as Austria, on our way to Zagreb, the Croatian capital. We were a little concerned that there might be problems getting our dog Rupert across the border checks into Slovenia and Croatia; the first borders which were manned since we had left Jersey. However, the guards paid little attention to us as they huddled in their guard-posts to keep out of the bitter cold.

We had been to Zagreb before so we were used to the busy roads with mostly old rusty cars and its similarity to a large mid-European city. Avoiding the many trams and trying to keep the car wheels from sticking in the tramlines was not a new experience but driving on the old cobbled streets in icy conditions was an added hazard requiring a great deal of concentration. We planned that on our drive down to Split we should stay at one of the hotels in the Plitvicka national park about three hours out of Zagreb. Plitvicka is quite high and is an area of forest, rivers, stunning waterfalls and lakes and is quite popular in the summer. We duly arrived there in very icy conditions just in time for dinner at the only hotel which was open. This was a typical product of the communist regime; a huge barn of a place, modern in style with no frills. Our bedroom and bathroom were enormous but quite basic. Nevertheless, everything was clean and tidy if a little worn. What was immediately noticeable was the number of staff everywhere; at reception, in the restaurant, bar and just walking about looking important. There were certainly far more staff than hotel guests. The restaurant, another great barn of a place, was warm and the staff very friendly. We were certainly well looked after and had a good wholesome meal of soup, steak and a large fruit pudding, washed down with a red Dalmatian wine.

Next morning we decided to walk down to the lake to see the waterfalls before setting off. We had been warned not to venture off the beaten track as the war had raged through that area and there were some areas which had not been cleared of mines. In addition, we were told: 'Watch out for bears'. Needless to say, with this advice ringing in our ears plus the bitter cold, the trip to the waterfalls was brief, but lovely. We certainly made a mental note to visit here again in warmer times.

The drive from Plitvicka to Split was quite an experience as it passed through a large part of Croatia which had been devastated during the recent Balkan war. The countryside was bleak and uninviting. Many of the villages were completely "bombed out" and only occupied by a few old people, all of whom seemed to be dressed in black .

We arrived in Knin, a substantial town, which had a large Serb population before the recent war, but they all had fled to Serbia when the Croatians advanced. Our son Mark had been an EU Monitor there during all the troubles and saw the ethnic cleansing at first hand. Now it looked poor and very much third world. After our travels through wealthy consumer orientated European countries on the way down to Croatia, this was a real culture shock.

March was getting worried and said: 'This is bandit country, what are we doing here!'

Fortunately, a short while after Knin the "ghost villages" thinned out and we saw a number of attractive looking café/bars spaced out along the route. Some were roasting whole sheep on an outside grill ready for the lunch trade. The nearer we got to Split the more civilised and cared for the villages became. After Sinj, which seemed to be a lively and more prosperous town, we descended from the hills to the busy ancient port of Split, with the Adriatic spread out before us and our Island of Brac in full view.

"THE BUTCHER"

Chapter 2

Food and Farmyard Impressions

After missing the 2pm ferry to Brac we had time to kill before the next one at 4.30. So we set off along the palm-lined promenade on the Split seafront in search of a late lunch. The Venetian architecture mixed with Roman ruins gave Split a very Italian flavour and the sun had brought out many people for a stroll. We found a restaurant and tucked into steak, 'Zagreb' style, stuffed with ham and cheese and coated with breadcrumbs; I suppose we would call it 'cordon-bleu'. Washed down with a couple of glasses of their red wine we were amazed at how cheap it was.

Duly refreshed we set off to catch the ferry. It was already getting dark when we boarded the 'Vladimir Nazor', an ancient old tub, though smartly painted in blue and white. In search of seats and warmth for the one-hour journey we found the bar, a dingy, smoky room reminiscent of the old British Rail station cafes, filled with noisy chattering Croatians.

The Croatians, like the Italians, talk very loudly and

frequently gesticulate and shout to emphasise a point. The bar was mostly full of large men (Croatians are quite a tall big race) with shaggy black hair and designer stubble, looking very much like a gang of bandits. We settled down in a corner with our drinks to watch and listen to the throng; March albeit, a little dubiously, as she found it all rather intimidating. However we soon realised that it was all good natured banter, though a bit loud, amongst a cheerful bunch of Islanders returning from work or shopping in Split.

The drive from Supetar, where we docked, to Povlja was across the centre of the Island which rises to almost the highest point of over 870m. Initially the road climbed very steeply around numerous tight bends until we levelled out, but by now it was dark and we had noticed sheets of ice covering the rocks and cliffs lining the route, an unusual sight for the Island, but ominous even so. The road was good, though there was some black ice, and we saw no more than two or three cars on the 40 km drive; later we were to discover that seeing as many as six cars was 'busy'!

At last we descended the hill to Povlja and saw the twinkling lights around the harbour. We found the house where Mr Zdinavic's friend Kruno held the key to our newly acquired home. Kruno showed us into our house, put on the electricity and asked us, through his daughter who spoke some English, why we had come in the Winter and not the Summer. Baffled, with much shaking of heads, they left us to it, probably muttering that the English were completely mad.

The house was freezing cold, with no heating, as

it had only ever been a Summer holiday home, and filled with old, basic Eastern-European type furniture, which was crammed into every spare bit of space. It had been agreed that it would be left in the house in case we wanted to buy some of it. First impressions were that it was all a load of hideous junk, but at least we had a bed and somewhere to sit. March was not at all happy.

'This is awful,' she said.

This was not a good beginning and I felt very guilty.

'I'm not staying here tonight' said March, 'Lets go to the hotel.'

'Good idea I said Humbly.'

At the well-lit hotel on the harbour front we found a member of staff, a small rotund middle-aged woman with dyed red hair, who promptly told us: 'No tourists!'

'What sort of a hotel is this?' we said. 'A hotel with no tourists!'

With her limited English she explained that the hotel was used by British soldiers from Bosnia, so that they could attend courses in sailing, diving, windsurfing and other recreational activities.

When I explained that I had stayed there the previous September, she repeated: 'No tourists!'

Thoroughly dejected we returned to our cold house. We sat in the lounge/diner and put the electric oven and electric hobs fully on in the kitchen, which was just through an archway, and held a council of war. In the mood we were in we decided that we had made a big mistake. March was in tears and I wasn't far from tears myself.

'We will do the place up over the next three months and sell it.' Said March.

I agreed. At least we had a solution and something to work for so it made us feel a little better.

Fortunately, March had packed not only bedding, including a duvet, but her faithful electric blanket. Having been brought up in the Yorkshire Dales in the fifties and experienced the cold winters there, and also serving 20 years in the regular army, cold sheets had not been a problem for me and indeed I used to have a weird masochistic pleasure in getting into a cold bed and waiting for the body to heat it up.

However, when March and I got together over 20 years ago, she introduced me to the duvet, another novelty for me and something I initially hated, because my feet seemed to want to spend the night sticking out the bottom. However in the interests of marital bliss I succumbed. The electric blanket was another matter. An ex military chap had to make a stand sometimes, so I insisted March had a single one on her side of the bed. This didn't last for long as I found myself on cold winter nights getting into bed and putting my feet over onto the warmth of her side, much to March's chagrin. It wasn't long therefore before a double electric blanket was acquired.

We were certainly grateful for it on that first cold night in Croatia.

'Thank God for your foresight,' I said.

We also had all our ski suits and our overcoats, which we piled on the bed, so that eventually a great feeling of pleasurable warmth lessened our misery as we cuddled together.

The next day greeted us with lovely sunshine but the temperature remained very cold. Our first resolve therefore was to seek out some electric fires. We set off for the next village called Selca, which had two hardware shops, which normally stocked electric fires, but they had of course all been sold. We were not aware at the time that we had arrived in Croatia during the worst winter they had had in 35 years. Our only hope therefore was the main port of Supetar where we had docked the day before, and which we were assured by the Selca shopkeepers would have electric fires, so we set off on the 40 km drive. We duly found an electrical shop and there we saw an electric fan heater.

'We'll have three of those,' I said hopefully.

'Ah problema' said the shopkeeper.

'Dis is de only one.'

At least we would have some warmth so we set off home a little happier, clutching our little heater!

On the way home we called into a small flower shop in Supetar and bought some flowers for our next-door neighbours to introduce ourselves. They had the Bistro/Pizzeria just behind our house and so far we had seen no sign of them. When we got home they were not in so we left the bunch of flowers on the doorstep with a note to introduce ourselves and went home to huddle round the new fire.

That evening just as we were finishing our meal there was a tap on the shutters to our French windows to the terrace. After I unlocked the shutters and doors we saw a young woman clutching a large plate covered in tinfoil, the cold wind swirling around her.

'Dis is for your pudding' she said and then introduced herself as Erika, our next-door neighbour.

She stayed for a glass of wine whilst we revealed the contents of the plate, which turned out to be six delicious hot pancakes with a tasty hot jam sauce. Erika, tall and pretty in her mid thirties, with large round eyes and a delightful grin, spoke very good English and chatted and joked cheerfully about the weather and our bad luck arriving in one of their worst winters in living memory. Little did we know that in the weeks and months to come Erika would be a great source of information about everything to do with living in Croatia and the Island in particular. Before she left we found out that their pizzeria would be open the following evening as they were open at weekends during the winter months.

We immediately reserved a table.

*

Buying food became our next challenge. So far we had been into the local small shop in Povlja and had found it not very well stocked with little of what we really wanted. We did however buy a few essentials, including bread, milk, frozen chicken pieces of which they had an abundance, eggs and pasta. The shop did not stock vegetables except onions, carrots and potatoes but at least we had enough to survive. We also discovered that the shop closed at noon and didn't reopen until 5pm, obviously due to the long hot summer afternoons, which were yet to come hopefully, if we survived the winter.

One thing we did find though was red wine and slivovic. We saw a little ground floor garage in a house along the harbour with the doors open and a chap buying wine from a large vat which was filling up plastic bottles. We shook hands with the owner, a man called Frani, who spoke to us in German. He was a big jovial, fit looking man in his 70's and he asked us what we wanted. I said I didn't have any bottles but would like a couple of litres of red wine. He then produced new plastic bottles and told us to use these every time we bought wine. When we got home we tried it and it was really very good.

"This is very drinkable. We are going to have to invest in more plastic bottles!" I said, wishing we had gone for more. Who knows when we were going to catch him there again.

We asked about meat and were told that there were two butchers in Selca, not 10 mins away, so we hurriedly drove there only to discover that both were shut and it was only 11.15 in the morning. There was no notice on the door as to opening times; obviously the locals didn't need to be reminded of this. We had also begun to wonder about vegetables as the two grocers shops in Selca also only stocked, guess what: potatoes, carrots and onions and we could not see any signs of a vegetable market; perhaps it was on certain days of the week only, we thought. Anyway we resolved to compile a list of questions to ask Erica that night, which couldn't come too quickly as far as we were concerned; things seemed to be going from bad to worse.

We arrived at the pizzeria at 8pm having wrapped up

against the cold of the night and walked the 40 yards or so, after being vetted by Erika and Robi's large German Shepard dog called Ruff. Passing through the outside stone tables we entered the restaurant's winter quarters and were greeted by an enormous log fire and Erika, who introduced her husband Robi. He greeted us with his beaming smile and loud voice:

'Gud eevenink neighbours.'

To me he looked very like Peter Sellars in his best Goon mode with his toothy grin, black bushy hair and heavy rimmed spectacles, behind which were those laughing eyes. We settled down next to the fire and warmed ourselves – this was heaven.

'Vot you vont drink?' asked Robi.

We ordered a large cherry brandy for March and a large glass of Dalmatian red wine for me, whilst we viewed the menu. The red wine, or 'black wine' as they call it, was superb; it was certainly as good as any table wine I had tasted in France. The restaurant only did pizzas in the winter but we had a very good selection from which to choose.

'Why you come here, you know, in vinter?' asked Robi smiling.

'We were told by Lucy that it was mild. Her parents only have one fire in the whole house.'

'Dey cold now,' laughed Robi.

'Dis vinter werry bad you know.'

After more drinks we tucked into the most delicious and enormous pizzas and then, armed with our list, questioned Erika and Robbi about living in Brac.

We discovered that the butcher opened from 7 to

11am and that vegetables could be obtained from vans and trucks which parked on the harbour in Povlja or on the square in Selca; what was uncertain was which days of the week so we would have to keep our eyes open. There were also markets every day in the resort of Bol and the port of Supetar but we were not keen to drive so far in such weather as by now we had sleet and the roads were becoming quite icy.

A few locals came in for a pizza or just a drink but mostly we had Erika and Robi to ourselves. They were eager to know all about us and also about what Britain was like and how we did things and Robi was keen to improve his limited English. Having paid the bill, amazingly only 100 kuna (under£10), we reluctantly tore ourselves away to our now much warmer house feeling that things were not so bad after all. We resolved that Saturday night would become our regular treat at the pizzeria. We also found as the weeks passed that the number of clientele increased as more locals and Erika and Robi's friends found us a novelty and wanted to ask us about England and the English.

Monday arrived so we shot off to Selca early to catch the butcher. Both butchers shops gave very little indication that they were shops at all; with only a small sign over the door (Mesnica) of what looked like an ordinary house and no window display and no meat to be seen anywhere in the shop!! This was like the John Cleese and Michael Palin cheese shop sketch in 'The Secret Policeman's Ball'. Having ascertained that they spoke neither English, German nor French, we knew we had a problem in ordering any meat at all; there wasn't even anything to point at.

In the end March took control and 'mooed' loudly.

The butcher's eyes lit up and he disappeared to a back room and brought out a big quarter of beef from which we chose some suitable cuts. March was not finished.

She then proceeded to both 'baa' and then 'cluck', including flapping elbow movements, until the right meat was brought from the back room. Her chicken impression was certainly worthy of an Oscar. The meat looked good and all the bones and fat were removed before weighing so we were well pleased. The butcher who had been a little surly at first had a broad smile on his face as he bid us farewell "dobar videnja, bog bog". (bog was a word they used a lot, meaning God)

'Bog bog,' we said and trotted off with our meat.

The sequel to this incident occurred that afternoon whilst March was pottering and taking stock in the garden, on a sunny though cold afternoon. She heard laughter coming from Erika and Robi's terrace, which overlooked our garden. Apparently the owner of the butchers, not the one who served us, had witnessed our visit and whilst visiting his friends Erika and Robi, related the tale of the animal noises from some mad Englishwoman. Whilst they were standing there he spotted March in the garden and exclaimed, "That's her!!"

Robi then proceeded to tell him that we were their friends so he had better make sure we were well looked after in the meat department.

As part of our search for a better selection of food we set off for Supetar one day to find a 'discount supermarket' which we had been told about. Just before Supetar we saw the sign 'Discount' in English and happily drove down the road to a large warehouse building. Something was wrong though as there were only two cars outside; perhaps they were closed. No, the door was open and we entered into a large barn of a warehouse full of racks and shelves, but alas most were empty and only a small section was stocked with food and other household goods. To say the least the actual quantity of food was no more than our little village shop had on the shelves. We left, after having a good look for anything new, as we would rather spend our money in the village if we could; the price was no better anyway so 'discount' was a bit of a misnomer.

We went on into Supetar to the vegetable market and also to buy a kettle if we could find one. The man in the electrical shop where we bought the fire spoke good English but had never heard of a kettle.

'Ketteel, vat is ketteel?'

We drew a picture and described in detail what a kettle was for but alas no luck. But he did think it was a good idea though. We found another shop in the town, which had a small display of electrical goods, but alas they had never heard of a kettle either. When we again described what it was for the female shop owner said:

'You don't need one of those. Ve boil water in a pan on stove, much better.'

We returned home to boil a pan of water for tea.

That evening in the fading light of day March called me from the garden to talk to an old man who was trying to get a message over to her. She thought he was asking for a heater for the cold. He could not speak much English but had a little German so I tried to get his drift. What he said was that the 'Bura' was coming during the night and did we have a fire to keep us warm.

'What is the Bura?' I asked apprehensively in German.

'It is the big wind from Siberia,' he replied.

I assured him we had a fire and would close the shutters and I thanked him for his concern. We hurried up to Erica and Robi who confirmed the Bura was coming and could last for a few hours or a few days.

'De Bura is known as de tidy lady,' said Erika. 'It blows all the leaves and rubbish into one corner of de garden.'

Apparently, it is possible to predict the Bura as it seems to arrive on the same days every year. For example, they told us, in the month of March it comes on the 7th, 17th and 27th. What was certain was that it would be very strong and it would be even colder.

That night we had a tap on the shutters and there again was Erika with a plateful of pancakes.

'To varm you up before the Bura', she said. She then noticed me in the kitchen cooking our evening meal.

'Mr Mike in kitchen,' she said to March. She appeared in the entrance.

'You are cooking!' she exclaimed. I then explained that it was a hobby of mine that I had taken up after leaving the army and that I now did most of the cooking.

'I must get Robi, he must see dis'. She then shot off and returned with Robi.

'Mr Mike. Vat you doing?' exclaimed Robi with a puzzled look.

'Ah, you cook!' he said with almost disbelief. 'I, no cook!'

'Don't tell men in willage you cook' he added sternly.

Apparently, Croatian men didn't cook unless it was their profession. Robi then glanced around the house and Erika, noticing this, said that they had never been invited into the house by the previous owner, in the 12 years he had owned it.

Later that night we went to bed and watched a video. We had brought a small TV and video but although we could get a perfect picture for Croatian TV we had no sound. This was probably because our TV was old and not 'multi standard'. We therefore became quite good at watching a silent John Wayne and trying to master lip reading. The Croatians have some excellent American and British films and TV programs, all with sub titles and not dubbed like the French and Germans do. We resolved to get a proper TV set but in the meantime we had the enjoyment of about a dozen videotapes, which we had brought with us. Some were films and others were four hour tapes of some of our favourite TV programmes such as 'Ello, Ello', 'Last of the Summer Wine', 'Dad's Army', 'The Fast Show' and 'Absolutely Fabulous' to name but a few of our library. After three months we had watched some of them two or three times. I think I can recite many of the sketches from 'The Fast Show' off by heart. March was also getting fed up with seeing 'Casablanca' (my favourite film) yet again. After our evening watching a video we fell asleep warm as toast from the electric blanket and the mounds of blankets and clothing piled on our bed and the comforting hum of our little fan heater.

At 2am I was awakened by a worried March.
'What on earth is that noise?' She exclaimed.
Still half asleep I felt I was on a railway station with a fast Inter-City Express hurtling past. It was the Bura. We had never experienced the Mistral in France but from what we had heard it must be something like the Bura. The wind was howling around the eaves and rattling the shutters on the seaward side of the house. We both agreed that we just had to see this! Pulling on trousers, shoes and warm overcoats we ventured out onto our terrace.

At first we were sheltered by the angle of the house to the wind and then as we peered round the wall towards the sea we were hit with the full force and coldness of it. I had experienced winds as strong as this in Jersey but on that night it seemed pretty awesome. It was a beautiful, clear, moonlit night and we could quite clearly sea the mainland 5 miles away and the endless white horses on the waves in between.

We could not stay there for long as the wind took our breath away so that it was difficult to breathe and we were beginning to feel the cold. So inside we went, shuttered up and did what most English people would do on such occasions, made a pot of tea and munched some delicious locally made biscuits we had purchased in the shop.

The next day was bright and sunny as it often is during a Bura, but there was no let up in the strength of the wind. Having been used to walking our dog on the beach in Jersey during strong winds, we spurned the car and set off on foot for some necessary groceries. We didn't see a soul and didn't know until much later that some of our neighbours had seen us and thought we were completely mad going for a walk in the Bura; something not done by the sensible people of Brac. We did however come across a lone runner, small, wiry and tough looking.

'Hello' he said with an English accent.

When we replied 'Good morning,' (we hadn't learnt the Croatian pleasantries by this time such as 'dobar dan' – good day) he said, 'You must be English' and stopped to talk. He turned out to be the British Army captain, from the Army Physical Training Corps, in charge of the training centre based on the hotel. We explained what we were doing in Povlja and invited him to drop in any time for a coffee or a beer (judging by his fitness and dedication to running in such weather, it was more likely to be a coke or a coffee. Quite unlike my days in the army!) He in return said that we were welcome to use the facilities of the hotel; they had a bar every evening and had Sky TV.

When we told him about our first night and the "No tourists" incident he was amused but appalled. He also agreed to let us have all the old newspapers, which would be a week old before we got them, but welcome anyway, particularly the gossip and the crosswords.

It wasn't long before we took up his offer by nipping in for a drink on the occasional night and to use their phone, which we could pay for at reception. The only other phones were outside the post office and on the hill near the church; both windy and cold places in the prevailing weather conditions, plus we had to remember to buy a phone card which was rapidly eaten up on international calls. March had been feeling a little cut off in a strange country and environment and had missed very much not being able to chat to her daughter Marika in Jersey on the phone. They were very close and apart from a good mother and daughter relationship they were great friends.

Sunday night in particular became a regular venue at the hotel where we had told our five grown up children we would be so that they could contact us if they wished. It was on our first Sunday night there that we met Suzy, a local girl who worked as a receptionist, and because of her excellent English was a great help to the army with translations and local knowledge. We were to get to know Suzy and her lovely family very well during the next weeks and months. On Sunday nights she was also running the small bar. She was soon aware that our orders were always cherry brandy and red wine.

*

That night, and every Sunday night, we also chatted

to some of the soldiers, who were over on a brief spell of recreational water sports, from their tours of duty in Bosnia. As we sat there in our warm Austrian overcoats in a rather chilly bar (the hotel owner was not inclined to turn up the heating for mere British soldiers, though the captain eventually managed to get her to sort out the heating in the hotel) sipping our drinks, we bemoaned the cold winter.

One Welsh lad chimed up, 'This is nothing. Back at our base in Bosnia we are living in containers with six foot of snow outside and only a paraffin heater to keep us warm'.

Things obviously hadn't changed much since I had left the Army 20 years before. However, soldiers expect to live in rough conditions; it's all part of the job. The British soldier is the most durable of any I know, and will put up with anything, remaining cheerful and loyal under conditions of adversity, but alas many are returning to Bosnia and Kosovo on repeat tours of duty on a regular basis at the government's bidding. No wonder it is difficult to retain soldiers in an army, which is so overstretched. You would certainly not get many other nation's soldiers prepared to live in those conditions without morale going to rock bottom.

It was like old times chatting to the soldiers in the bar and hearing about their experiences in Bosnia. It was a welcome short break for them to come to Povlja and enjoy the water sports, climbing and mountain-biking in spite of the cold.

"THE MAN FROM IMOTSKI" & HIS FURNITURE!

Chapter 3

The Man from Imotski

It wasn't long before Mr Zdinjvic wanted to come to collect his furniture and to ask if we wished to buy any of it. Originally, we thought that we had bought the house complete with furniture, but there must have been a misunderstanding at the lawyers' office, as our son Mark phoned to say Mr Zdinjvic wanted money.

He arrived with his wife, a short, timid and plain woman, who was dressed in her Sunday best of a black trouser suit, white blouse and gold shoes, with her dyed blonde hair recently permed. However, this did not deter her from racing through the house sweeping and cleaning frantically. We told her that this was not necessary, not that either of them spoke any English, nor we Croatian, though she understood our sign language. She nevertheless pressed on with her cleaning with gusto. As we had mentioned that we might be interested in the double bed and a couch, Mrs Zdinjvic was also scribbling down prices of all the furniture and having hushed conversations with her husband in between him loading all their stuff from the garage.

Eventually they were ready. We settled down on the terrace in the winter sun and Mr Zdinjvic, with his friend's daughter from the village acting as a translator, asked for 1200 Deutschmarks (DMs) for all their furniture. They always conducted business in DMs and not in their own currency. We paid for the house in DMs and have since asked for building quotes, which were given in DMs. They obviously have little confidence in their own Kuna or the euro which came in that year.

March and I had already discussed the prices we were prepared to pay for various items so we were amused by this rather ridiculous asking price. The furniture was all very old, but could hardly be classified as antique. It was communist utilitarian, and not in good condition. Some of it, particularly the enormous wardrobes, had hideous designs in the veneer; the wardrobe doors in fact looked as though they had complete crocodile skins embedded in them. I looked suitably amazed and said through the girl interpreter that it was only worth half that, but we were not interested in all of it, only the bed and the table and chairs. I offered him 200 DMs for these items.

It was then that Mr Zdinjvic's demeanour changed from the jovial round schoolteacher to that of a hard-bitten mountain bandit, which he more readily resembled. He was not happy, his moustache twitched and he grew even redder in the face. I thought we were going to have an international incident as he was obviously offended, so I quickly said that we were not being rude about his furniture, we just didn't want it and he could take all of it away. Where we were going to eat and sleep if he took it all away I wasn't sure, as we had not even got round to exploring furniture shops, even if there were any on the island. In the end he took quite a lot away on his car and trailer to store in his friend's house in the village and he would return the next weekend for the rest. Fortunately he didn't take the bed so at least we had somewhere to sleep! We also had a lot more room to move around the house.

We had to find a furniture shop fast. We asked Robi and Erika who said there was one in Supetar, which was about 40 minutes drive away. We set off on the next day and with a little sketch map we eventually found the shop in a backstreet on the outskirts of the town in the middle of a housing estate. They had, amazingly, quite a selection of furniture and bathroom and kitchen units. We found a really super big wooden double bed, which was far bigger than we had been used to, but it was just what we wanted. We also bought matching bedside cupboards and a large matching wooden framed mirror. The girl in the store was very friendly and spoke quite good English. She said they would deliver the next day and that we would get 10% discount if we paid cash to the driver on delivery. Unfortunately there was nothing there to buy for the living room, but at least we had made a start. As this was the only furniture store on the island we knew we would have to go over to Split in search of other items.

As we came out of the store we noticed another shop

almost hidden round the corner. It was an ironmonger's store rather like I remembered from the fifties; the sort of place that sold absolutely everything. It was certainly reminiscent of the shop in the TV programme the "Two Ronnie's ", in the sketch where Ronnie Barker asks for "forkandles" and gets fork handles but really wants four candles – I think that was it – anyway this shop had everything from garden equipment, all sorts of tools, pet food and a multitude of hardware, though only one or two of each. This was a find, but also the dog food looked much better than the food in our village store. He didn't seem to have an electric kettle though and I wasn't even going to try to ask him about that!

*

On arriving back in Povlja we met Suzy, the girl we had met in the hotel, whilst having a coffee in a little bar on the harbour and we related our tale of the furniture. She told us of a very large furniture store on the outskirts of Split. We resolved to go there after the bed was delivered. The next day a truck appeared with a pleasant young man who I helped to offload the bed and carry the dissembled parts to our bedroom. He then proceeded to unpack it and assemble it all; all part of the service. I paid him the cash and offered him a tip, which he refused. Amazing. The bed had solid, arched headboard and tailboard and was sprung with strong arched laths in two frames. The mattress was of good quality and very comfortable and all at about half the price we would have paid in Jersey.

After a comfortable night in our new enormous bed we set off early next morning for the 6am ferry from Sumartin to Makarska, on the mainland coast. Makarska is about an hours drive from Split, but although this was not the most direct route to Split, the store was more easily approached from Makarska. We were also looking forward to the drive along the coast road. The ferry took an hour and as anticipated the drive was as spectacular as the Italian coast around Sorrento and Positano. The road skirted the high mountains along the coast and went through pretty little fishing villages with all the tourist boats in the harbour having their winter maintenance before the onset of summer. We stopped for a coffee as we approached Split in a little restaurant, which had a glorious view of the sea and our island of Brac. Although the air was crisp the January sunshine made us feel good.

It wasn't long before we found the furniture store, which was visible from the main road. It was four stories high and was crammed with furniture. As we worked our way from floor to floor we looked at one another realising that there was little there that was to our liking.

March's comment was: ' I feel as though we are on the film set of Dr Who, it is all rubbish!'

It was all updated Zdinjvic-type furniture. Multicoloured crocodiles seemed to infest all the veneer and much of it was black and shiny. We were after minimalist, Mediterranean style. Chrome and glass was also in vogue much the same as Britain in the sixties and G Plan seemed to have just reached Croatia. On the top floor we at last found something to our liking.

It was a 'stuberl' just like the ones you see in Austrian houses; with an attractive wooden, padded corner seat to seat four and a table and two chairs. But alas, the shop assistant said: 'Ah, problema, no deliver to Brac.'

We were going to have to find some way of getting it to Brac, but we decided to take the ferry back from Split to Supetar and ask the furniture store in Supetar if they could get hold of a stuberl. We just made it in time as the store closed at 3pm. I tried to explain to the girl what we wanted, she didn't understand stuberl so I drew a diagram.

'Ah, she said, a kutna klupa'!

She then pulled out several catalogues and we thumbed through them. Then at last we saw the kutna klupa, in fact loads of them in all shapes and sizes. We selected one and she phoned her head office on the mainland.

'One week' she said.

We were beginning to get things together and returned home well satisfied. True to their word the Kutna klupa arrived a week later and we had great fun assembling it from the flat-packs.

*

Mr Zdinjvic, on his next visit arrived with his friend from the village, plus his friend's daughter as interpreter and began to remove the furniture to his friend's house. Then, all of a sudden his friend produced tools and went into the kitchen.

'What are you doing?' I asked through his daughter.

'He is taking out all the kitchen units' she said.

'No he isn't!' I replied and shooed them out of the kitchen.

We then had a heated discussion on what was furniture and what were fittings. He fully intended to take out all the units including the sink unit, complete with taps and water heater and was most insistent that they were furniture. We were quite happy that he took the fridge and cooker as they were both old and the cooker's gas fittings didn't work anyway, but we decided to "dig in" over the fitted units.

'Does this mean that you are going to remove all the bathroom units and lavatory as well?' I asked.

'No' was the reply, somewhat sheepishly. 'Bathroom is different'.

This logic somewhat defeated us so I telephoned our son Mark to ask him to speak to the lawyers to ask who was right. Unfortunately, it was Saturday afternoon and they were not available even on their mobiles, so we had stalemate. All the furniture was duly removed whilst I stood guard at the kitchen door, as I was sure they would make another attempt.

Parting with Mr Zdinjvic was somewhat cool. He told us through the girl that in Croatia they did things differently and that our "anglo saxon" logic was not valid there. He said he would return next weekend once the matter was cleared up with the lawyers.

Our son Mark phoned on the Monday to say that he had spoken to the lawyers, who said that it was generally not done to remove fitted kitchen units but as it had not been mentioned in the contract, and as there was no law governing such matters, we would have to reach an agreement with Zdinjvic.

Thoroughly miffed we decided to buy two of the Kitchen units and we would replace the rest hopefully within the week. So off to our friendly furniture store in Supetar where they had everything we needed in stock. A busy week of fitting it all together including all the plumbing of the sink lay ahead, but in the end it was good to have largely our own units and not someone else's.

In the meanwhile Zdinjvic had got hold of Mark's number in Zagreb and had been pestering him and complaining about us over the furniture charade. He said that when he arrived the next Saturday he didn't want March there, not just because he claimed she had been rude about his furniture, but because in Croatia men do all the dealings on such matters. He also said he wanted some money to cover his expenses for this extra trip.

"Think again chum" I said, but he obviously didn't understand but I could see he got the drift!

We told Erika and Robi about the saga and they were amazed and appalled. They had never heard of fitted units being removed and were even more astounded to hear he wanted money for expenses. They then told us that people from Imotski, located in a remote part of Croatia on the Bosnian border, were more Bosnian than Croatian and were hard sheep-farming stock and had their character moulded by the grim and rocky landscape of the region. They were hard and uncompromising; Zdinjvic was true type. We did however have a laugh as we decided to christen him "The man from Imotski".

Robi said that he would come down as interpreter and March could wait with Erika in their house.

'His head like rock, you know!' laughed Robi.

The man from Imotski duly arrived on the Saturday in his old Mercedes (everyone in Imotski has an old Mercedes Robi later told me). I had put all his units etc, near to the main gate so that he didn't have far to carry them. I had decided to be pleasant as I wanted the matter closed. Robi had other ideas. He was incensed at the price the man from Imotski wanted for the two units and even more incensed over the travel expenses. Robi harangued him in his loud Croatian voice, shouting and gesticulating, and generally giving him a very hard time. The man from Imotski remained as solid as the rock from his region. Robi could make no indentation.

'He is mad!' said Robi in frustration.

In the end I paid the price for the units and gave him half of what I thought his expenses were. He wasn't happy, but when I said through Robi that was all he was getting, he reluctantly agreed and we shook hands on the matter. He did however make a passing comment, with Robi interpreting, that:

'All the fuss was caused by "Anglo-Saxon" logic, which has no place in Croatia', and

'These foreigners come here and try to tell us what to do.'

He then, unbelievably, strode up to Robi's house saying that he wanted to say goodbye to March!

March was having a drink with Erika's sister Ada and her husband Emir, a Muslim from Bosnia and a very amusing and entertaining man with an evil wit. Amazingly the man from Imotski said to March that we were very welcome to visit them in Imotski and to stay in their house!

'In the next hundred years!' quipped Emir, and with that the man from Imotski gritted his teeth and stormed off, hopefully never to darken our door again.

*

Two days after the man from Imotski incident, our pipes froze. It was actually a bright sunny morning, as indeed most of January had been, but this morning had a real bite to it. I searched the house to see any signs of burst pipes and then tried to work out where the pipes might have frozen. The house was reasonably warm with our two electric heaters so I was sure it was not in the house. The water system, like most continental countries, is a direct mains system to all the taps, with no tank in the roof like we have, so at least I didn't have to scramble about in the roof.

I traced the mains pipe through the garage, which is below the house, and up into the bathroom. I decided to heat up the garage with our electric fire, convinced that this was where they had frozen. Whilst going back through our garden, still in my dressing gown and with a grim countenance, Robi leaned over the garden wall.

'Hey neighbour – problem?'

'Our pipes have frozen,' I said meekly.

'Ah, temperature minus 11C', he said shaking his head knowingly.

'But perhaps problem, you know, is under garden vere pipe go', said Robi grinning.

This I had not considered. If he was right the sun may thaw out the pipe.

We got dressed and did the best we could with our ablutions with what we had in the kettle and sauntered into the village to do a bit of shopping. Thank heavens for our Austrian overcoats and woollen ski hats because the cold was biting. Passing the hotel we saw Keith, the army captain, who when he heard of our burst pipes insisted we move into the hotel at once! We thanked him and said that we certainly would if the pipes had not defrosted before the end of the afternoon. They hadn't and we so moved in.

That evening we had a traditionally British meal with the soldiers who looked robust and red faced after a day on their various recreational pursuits in the cold. Soup, followed by roast pork, crackling, roast potatoes and vegetables, and finished off with apple pie and custard, was just what was required to warm us up and pick up our morale. Having frozen pipes didn't seem so bad after all.

After chatting to the soldiers over a few drinks in their freezing cold bar (a glass conservatory on the side of the hotel), we retired to a warm bedroom and hoped for some good luck the next day.

We were indeed lucky. It was another sunny day but the temperature had risen to above freezing so by lunchtime we had water again. I was concerned with the pipes defrosting that we might get a burst but we were lucky. Robi was probably right, the frozen pipe may well have been just under the topsoil of our garden.

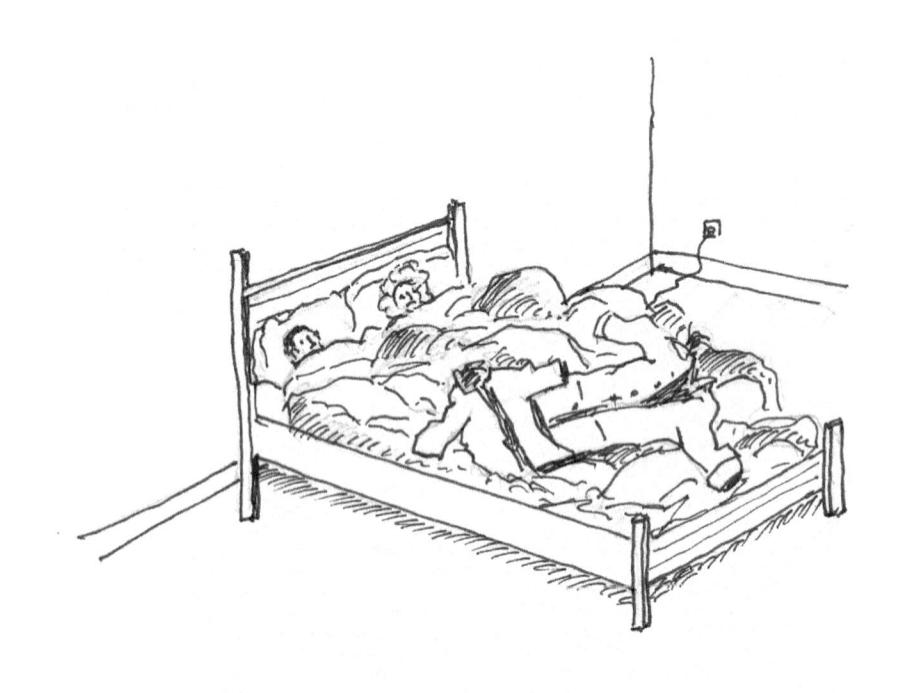

POULJIAN CENTRAL HEATING!

Chapter 4

The Dalmatians, and Monika Lewinski

We were beginning to meet many more people both in the village of Povlja and Selca nearby. Everybody was extremely friendly and helpful. They had very little money; the average wage was only £180 per month, 30% of the workforce was unemployed and there was no dole. So how they managed was at first a mystery particularly as the shops were almost as expensive as Jersey, except for meat, which was cheap. But we did discover that they managed quite well, through self-sufficiency, bartering and doing 'deals'. Also somewhere in the family there would be a vegetable garden, a fishing boat and an olive grove.

They are simple straightforward people who are content merely to have enough to live, simply and comfortably. Although many were out of work, they often worked "on the black". For example, just about every small builder, and there are a lot of them, is working unofficially in the black market.

We expected them to be Latin in their looks, rather

like the Italians, Greeks and Spanish, but they are quite different. Many of them, both men and women, are quite tall and handsome. The women in particular are tall and slim, with long black hair and always well dressed; what little money they have seems to go on smart clothing of the latest fashion. It was almost like watching a fashion parade when sitting in a cafe on the seafront in Makarska or Split with all the pretty girls parading up and down.

On one occasion, March who is quite tall, said: 'How unfortunate, that girl must be over six foot three!'

But she soon realised that a lot of them were like that. We were told by a Croatian friend that originally the Croats migrated from Persia to Poland, but the Romans pulled them down south as a buffer against the Mongol hoards. It certainly explained their different looks. They were the southern slavs, or Jugoslavs in their language.

We noticed in the cafes and bars that they would make an espresso coffee or a small beer last for well over an hour which made it a cheap form of entertainment. Not good turnover for the cafes, but the waiters never hurried people to vacate tables. Their cafes were always full as they are very much a café society who likes to chat and watch people go by.

We noticed that a lot of business is conducted in the many cafes, whether it is just a simple 'deal' of buying and selling something, or a proper business transaction. Many businessmen don't have an office – they take their briefcase and mobile phone to a café and meet people and operate from there. Card games are also very popular in cafes. There would always be a table with men playing cards from about 10am to midday when they would dash home for the meal their wives had slaved over to get cooked on time. Card games were also quite noisy with a lot of loud banter and rapping of knuckles on the table when they put down a card. This might have seemed good for business but the players usually made one small espresso last 2 hours!

*

One day we met Suzy, who worked at the hotel, and she took us to her grandmother's house and introduced us to her family. Cakes were brought out with a variety of home made schnapps and aperitifs. Living in the house was her grandmother Franika, her mother Nadia and father Toni. She also lived there with her small son Mario. We were to be invited on many occasions to their happy home. It was on that first occasion though that we were told about an Englishman who lodged with them in the 1960s during the old communist regime. The Englishman had claimed to be a writer and became very friendly with the young Nadia. One day he announced that he wanted to take her back to England. However, shortly after that the police arrived and found a radio transmitter in his room and the Englishman was arrested as a spy.

'I can assure you that we are not spies,' I said.

Franika clutched my hand with her strong old hands in a tight grip and said something with a big grin.

'She say, I'm sure you no spy,' translated Suzy.

We asked them if they knew an electrician in the village as we had some switches to be moved, the kitchen hot water heater to be wired-in and some of the plugs and lights didn't work.

Suzy chimed in:' My father is an electrician, he will happily do the work'.

Her father Toni, though retired on the meagre pension they have, did lots of odd jobs, including car repair. As Toni spoke no English we arranged for Suzy to bring him to our house the next day to see what was required. He worked for three days and sorted out all our problems. When we asked Suzy how much we owed him she showed us a small bill for electrical bits, about £1.50.

'What about his time?' I enquired.

'Oh, that is no charge as you are our friends' said Suzy.

'But we have only known you for such a short time, we must give him something!'

But Suzy was adamant that we didn't need to pay. I noticed that Toni was a smoker so I noted the brand and later bought him two large packs of cigarettes.

One amusing incident occurred whilst Toni was working on our electrics. I had been a professional artist for a few years so I had decided to brighten up our bedroom. I had therefore painted a mural above our bed head, consisting of a large garland held up by two cherubs, (a la Sistine chapel), to match March's curtains she was making. Toni was both fascinated and impressed by this and on his last day working for us he brought two of his card-playing chums from the village to show them the wall. They too were most impressed uttering many oohs and aahs. As this was not the last mural I had in mind for the house I expected that we would have much interest from the village folk.

*

One evening we had a visit from Lucy and her uncle Tonko. They had found the house for us and were calling to see how we were getting on. Tonko had retired and returned to Povlja after 35 years working in Vienna. He spoke no English but my rusty German got us by even though he had a strong Austrian accent. Tonko was a keen wine buff and had his own little vineyard. He also had a large olive grove above the village.

He had brought a bottle of his own red wine, or black wine as they call it, and a bottle of his own olive oil. The wine was excellent and we later discovered that he had won awards against well-known French vineyards. The olive oil was good enough to eat on its own. We were pleased to have the bottle as there was virtually no olive oil for sale in the shops, and what there was on the shelf was imported and not Dalmatian. The reason for that was that all the oil they make from their olive groves is for their own consumption. The local home made oil was certainly the best we had ever tasted. We did hear that the USA was keen to buy all the olive oil from Croatia that they could lay their hands on. It didn't look as though that would be much unless they had another source.

The Island of Brac used to be a major wine producing area early in the last century but the vines were devastated in the 1920s by the same disease, which struck the French vineyards in the 1890s. The vineyards never recovered, particularly on Brac, and the people left in their droves to seek their fortunes elsewhere in the world; the Island's population in the early 1900s was 26,000 but now is only 13,000. The old terraced vineyards have now largely been replaced by olive groves. However, there is now wine produced in Bol and also along the Dalmatian coast and I can testify to the fact that it is very good.

The next day we ventured into the village to have a coffee in one of the bars and met Tonko there. We saw an old fisherman walking along the harbour followed by a young lamb. We had actually seen both of them many times before and he had even taken the lamb for a walk out at the Punta near our house. We laughed and pointed them out to Tonko. 'Who is that old chap with the lamb?' I asked.

Tonko explained in German that for some time and some strange reason the old fisherman had been known as 'Clinton', so that when he appeared with his pet lamb, the villagers christened her 'Monika Lewinsky'.

We fell about laughing and immediately emailed all the family when we got home.

After a few weeks we didn't see the lamb anymore so Monika must have been ready to eat.

Apart from Robi and Erika who lived behind us, and the lady who lived next door called Lijeka, a retired biologist, the rest of our neighbours were weekenders from Split. They would arrive on Friday evening and depart on the very early ferry on Monday mornings. These were just passing acquaintances that we would wave to and pass the time of day. One couple had a boxer dog, so we referred to them as Mr and Mrs Boxer. One weekender though was the only miserable unsociable person we came across in Povlja. He obviously didn't like foreigners as he never acknowledged our 'dobar dans' (good day) so we nicknamed him Mr Grumpy. His wife however was very friendly so it seemed unfair to refer to her as Mrs Grumpy.

We continued to do work on the house. As the sun was out most days and the severe cold had gone we decided to attack the shutters, which were in need of attention. These we stripped and stained, a laborious and lengthy task, which took both of us several days to finish. We also found in the garage all the guttering and down pipes, which the Man from Imotski had never bothered to put up in the 12 years since the house had been built, so they had to go up. We were also busy weeding and sorting out the garden when one day Robi leaned over his terrace and said:

'Are all English like you?'

'Well we all do have similar characteristics', said March.

'No' said Robi, 'I mean, you know, do English all work like you? You do more jobs in one day than I do in month!'

We decided to take up the lino in most of the house and lay tiles so we went off to go tile hunting. There was nothing in the local hardware store in Selca we liked and he would have to order them from the mainland anyway, so there was nothing for it but to go to Makarska or Split. The early morning ferry to Makarska was at 6 am and took one hour so we arrived in Makarska at 7am on a still dark cold morning. However, the cafes were open so we enjoyed a breakfast of coffee and a Dalmatian version of the French croissant, before exploring the town for tile shops. Amazingly the first one we found had a good selection of tiles in stock and one in particular we liked very much; a Spanish tile with a shiny white marbled finish – ideal for scorching hot summers. We managed to get enough tiles into our estate car to do three rooms but she was well down on the springs!

On the way back to the harbour we saw a sign saying "VIP Card". This we knew to be a newly established mobile phone company who installed a simcard on a pay as you go basis; and the top up cards were available at all post offices. We had our old mobile phone in the car so we had it converted to VIP with a £20 credit on the phone as a starter. This was going to be better than the trips to the hotel telephone or the windy call boxes.

We immediately phoned all our children to let them know our number and they were greatly relieved to know that they could contact us. The additional advantage of VIP was that even though we were out of credit at any time people could still ring us and we could still dial the emergency numbers.

'I feel much happier now that we can use the mobile,' said March'

'I agree darling. It's a bit weird on some country roads with no villages or telephones around.'

After a light lunch at a harbour café and purchase of vegetables at the large and well-stocked fruit and vegetable market in Makarska, we were ready to board the ferry back to the island. However with our heavy load of tiles we almost ripped off the exhaust on the ferry ramp so that it then had that awful deep throated noise all the way home sounding like a main battle tank on manoeuvres. Robi heard us driving up to the house and leant over the garden wall.

'What you do?' he grinned

'Damaged the exhaust on the ferry,' I replied.

'Vait, I hev.' He said as he disappeared into the house'

'Dis special for exhausts.'

Robi handed me a tin of exhaust paste which with some wire did a reasonable first aid job until we could get to a garage.

"Thank you Robi, you're a gem".

"What gem?" he said.

"A really good friend ", I replied.

We were now ready to tile the floors so we pulled up the old lino, rolled it up and took it to the large euro bin not far from our house and left it alongside. Later that day March called me to say: 'Look over there at that house, those people are taking in our old lino!' We were pleased that it was being put to good use as it was still in reasonable condition but we did name the couple, who were weekenders from Split, Mr and Mrs Lino.

We had told Robi and Erika of our nicknames for all the

people around and they were highly amused and in fact from that day on proceeded to use the same nicknames. They did however have a different variation on Mr and Mrs Lino who they called Mr and Mrs Linoleum.

The tiling took about a week. I had done a bit before so I and found it quite an enjoyable task in spite of the inconvenience of not being able to tread on the tiles until set. Whilst the kitchen was out of action we ordered takeaway pizzas from Robi and Erika and munched them in the bedroom whilst watching 'silent' TV.

We decided to celebrate our new floors by inviting Robi and Erika and her mother and father to Saturday lunch. Her parents were a lovely couple who spoke no English but Erika kept pace with translations. Her mother had recently recovered from a heart bypass operation and was suffering from a problem with her leg and this showed on her countenance; at 62 she looked much older. During the lunch her parents were intrigued to know how old we were. March said she was 62, but looked much younger. However, when March said that I was 58, Erika put her hands to her mouth and exclaimed: 'OH, MISS MARCH!!!'

The thought that March had a "toy boy" really tickled them.

The incident was also amusing for us because Robi and Erika had always called us Mr Mike and Miss March, and in spite of our protestations to call us simply Mike and March, they never have.

March was a little nervous having them to lunch this first time as Erica and her mother had the reputations of being the best cooks in the village, as we were later to discover on many occasions. We did a huge lasagne and had found a lettuce from a visiting vegetable truck. So March did her famous (amongst family and friends) French dressing. Erika and her mother loved the dressing and insisted that March wrote down the recipe for them right away.

They also loved the apple pie and cream to follow. Apple pie was something they had never seen or tasted before nor our pastry. Little did we know at the time this was the start of an enthusiasm for recipe swapping between us all. This included emails when we were away from Povlja and requests to bring items, which they could not get. The fact that I cooked became a bit of an ongoing joke. Whenever Erika came to the house I always happened to be in the kitchen.

'Ah, Mr Mike cooking again. What you cook?' she would say with a laugh.

She was fascinated with some of the different things we ate. There, food was generally quite plain but wholesome. They had never experienced curries, Chinese stir-fry, chilli concarne (though we couldn't get the red beans there), coq au vin or some of the French style cooking I generally indulged in, when I could get the ingredients there or remembered to take a stock with me. They were not too sure they liked the hot and spicy food but the rest they seemed to enjoy. One cold Sunday in February I was cooking roast pork and also some Yorkshire puddings. Erika was having a glass of wine with us and I was trying to explain what Yorkshire puddings were.

'Well they are sort of puddings to have with meat,

made with pancake batter.' (This was going to be like trying to explain the finer points of cricket).I said that I would take a couple up to them when they were ready.

I took them up with some of the meat gravy and left them there whilst I dashed back to enjoy my Sunday lunch.

When we saw Robi and Erika later, Robi said:

'Vat this puddink? Werry nice but not puddink, because you eat with meat and gravy!!'

We were totally unable to explain to him why they were called puddings when most other puddings are desserts.

'English language werry strange', said Robi.

'Look, vat zis "Mary go round"?'

'Oh, you mean "merry go round", said March, who then described the carousel which children rode on at fairs.

Robi shook his head from side to side and said: 'I no understand why Mary go round and round and vat she do it for!'

We all had a good laugh at Robi's expense.

We were becoming much better known in the village with everybody referring to us as "The English" and greeting us as we strolled around. The girl at the little post office would dash out on every occasion we had mail to hand it to us personally as we walked past. If we had not walked in to the village on a day we had mail she would walk out to our house in the afternoon and deliver it personally, even during a Bura.

We were also venturing into one or two of the bars at

night to brighten up the long winter evenings. One of them, the Dok, was a warm and comfy little place with beer and wine at incredibly cheap prices. We also tried some of the Croatian aperitifs such as plinkovac, which was slightly bitter but nevertheless tasty, and their plum brandy sljivovica, which had quite a kick. The owner of the Dok was a thickset cheerful chap with a shaved head and a Balkan droopy moustache. He could certainly have played the bad man in some detective thriller, or even Kojak, but in fact was a nice friendly chap. He was a friend of Robi and Erika and had been Robi's best man at their wedding. We could never pronounce his name so we nicknamed him Mr Dok, in line with our other nicknames.

It was at the Dok one night that we met a Dutch couple, who we knew of as they had apparently wanted to buy our house, but had tried to get it much cheaper. The man from Imotski however had stuck to his price. They had been visiting Povlja on holidays for 15 years but were now intending to set up a water sports centre with a restaurant. They had sold their apartment in Holland and had another Dutch partner, or rather backer, in the venture. They told us of the immense paperwork and bureaucracy involved in setting up the business and getting the land. They were renting an apartment and fully intended to see it all through; a brave thing to do in a foreign country so different in its laws and ways from the rest of Western Europe. They also did not speak much of the language so Mr Dok was helping them out with translations.

They had great plans for the village, but we would have to wait and see whether this was genuine or just talk.

*

We decided to ask around for anyone who would take on the job of cleaning our house after our visits, washing sheets and towels, getting the place ready for our arrival and perhaps keeping the garden tidy. After a while Suzy said that her grandmother would do it. We were a little worried as Franika, who although she looked fit and quite tough, was 78 and might find it too much for her. However, she was most insistent and turned up early the next morning to see what was required.

She not only accepted the job but then went into the garden and started to weed and prune the trees and bushes until lunchtime. We offered tea and coffee and other refreshments from time to time but she refused and pressed on. This was far more than we expected and we were becoming a little embarrassed that Suzy's family were doing so much for us and we were unable respond in kind.

We then hit upon the idea of taking them all out to dinner as this was something they would not normally be able to afford. We discovered that most restaurants were closed in the winter but some did open at weekends and one, "The Petrovac," was high above the hill overlooking Selca and the port of Sumartin. Although we went at night we could see all the lights of these villages and the lights along the mainland coast. It was a charming setting with the moon also shining on the sea. There were seven of us altogether and apart from two other couples we had the restaurant to ourselves. The restaurant was fairly new and had been built by a millionaire just before the war there in the 90s when they had plenty of tourists. It had magnificent marble floors, the dance floor in verte antique was particularly striking. There was a colourfully lit waterfall cascading down a series of highly polished sections of stalagmites and the ceilings were beautifully panelled in wood with timber beams fanning out from a central point. The décor and pictures were good and the whole effect very pleasing and welcoming.

The waiter, who Suzy's family all knew, was smartly dressed and spoke good English. He placed bread on the table and also both iced and room temperature jugs of water; a custom which sadly many of our restaurants have forgotten. We ordered aperitifs and studied the menu, which was in four languages.

Everybody had starters, main course and dessert with several bottles of red wine, followed by coffee and schnapps. I remember I had an octopus salad to start, followed by an enormous mixed grill with beef, pork, lamb and spicy sausages with a mixed salad. I struggled to eat the dessert, which was a fruit tart. The food was excellent and the price astounding as the cost was only just over £50 for all of us. Suzy and her family enjoyed themselves and we told them over the coffee that this was just a small thank you for all the help and friendship they had given us.

"MONIKA LEWINSKI"

Chapter 5

Cream Paint

We still had a lot more work to do on the house. The house had three walls surfaced in Brac stone, a lovely creamy white colour, but the side of the house away from the sea had been rendered in dull grey cement with just some stonework around the archway to the door. The terrace walls were also similarly rendered and looked quite ugly compared to the rest of the house so we had to do something about painting them. The villagers had painted their rendered walls in white but we felt that this was too stark against the creamy coloured Brac stone so we decided on cream. The next trick was to find a cream paint.

We set off to Selca to see the little man with the small hardware shop where we had bought the stain for the shutters. He didn't have very much paint at all and what he had was all white; white gloss, white emulsion and white distemper. There was not a coloured paint in the place. We said that we wanted cream paint for our walls but he shook his head.

'No cream paint, only white. Everybody use white paint for walls', he said knowingly.

'Where can we get cream paint?' I said getting frustrated.

He shrugged his shoulders and gestured as if I was asking the impossible.

'Perhaps Split', he said.

We could always make a day trip to Split but I couldn't believe that there was no cream paint on the island. We departed from the shopkeeper who looked somewhat disappointed, as we had always bought something from him on our previous trips. He was a nice chap who had always been very helpful with our other purchases. Unusually small with a cheerful face he spoke to us in a mixture of broken English with some German thrown in with a good deal of sign language. Sign language, which was new to us was widely used there and was something we started to enjoy. He often only had one item of something on the shelf, but when we had needed more he had always had it down within a couple of days from the mainland store. We always seemed such a novelty to him, he probably had not met any English before.

He shook us by the hand as he always did and said:

'White paint much better for house – cream won't last'.

Followed by, 'Bog bog'.

'Bog bog,' we replied.

As always, we then consulted Robi and Erika when we had a problem. Robi chimed in with: 'Why cream paint, everybody have white!'

'We know,' said March. 'But we want cream paint. The English like cream paint and we want to be different.'

Robi laughed.

'You go Bol, you know, maybe cream paint dere.'

So we decided to combine our trip to Bol with a visit to a linen shop there. We had bought some sheets in the small shop in Selca but as usual they had only one of everything. Linen there is very high quality and very cheap so we were not only looking to buying for the Povlja house but our house in France, if we ever found one!

We set off on the 24-kilometre journey to Bol, which was the main tourist resort on the Island, but in February it was not likely to have many tourists. It was a lovely sunny day, although a little cold out of the sun, but we enjoyed the drive across the centre of the island, which rises quite high with terrific views. The road took us through Gornji Humac (which we had renamed "Horny Gumac" much to everybody's amusement) with the usual lack of traffic and enjoyed the drive on the empty roads. However, when you do meet a car it is going at breakneck speed. How they got their old wrecks to go so fast amazed us. Like the French, the Croatians are laid back people but when they get into a car they think they are all Michael Schumacher, without the same skill of course, and drive far faster than is really safe.

The drivers on Brac also must have been frustrated Englishmen as they invariably came round the corners on the left hand side of the road. They had also acquired that very annoying continental driver's habit of driving on your tail if you are going too slowly for them; very

French, in particular.

After "Horny Gumac" the road started to descend to Bol. The view from the top of the hill overlooking the sea and the Island of Hvar was quite stunning and reminiscent of the Italian coast around Amalfi, but with far more islands dotted about, some quite small but others like Hvar were quite large. The road was steep and winding, descending about five hundred metres to Bol, which nestles in close to the steep cliffs. March encouraged me to go slowly, as she did not like roads with a steep drop at the sides, and some of the bends did not have crash barriers.

The sea was calm with the occasional fishing boat pottering about between the islands, unlike the summer when there would be many tourist boats and yachts. Seen from well above the town the most striking feature of Bol is the famous beach, which appears on all the brochures of Dalmatia. It stretches out from a promontory containing most of the large hotels and looks like a long curved creamy beak in a beautifully clear green and blue sea. In the summer tourist months of July and August, the beach is packed with sun worshippers and bathers. Like most of Dalmatia's beaches, which are largely rocky, it has no sand but consists of fine particles of stone. This is one feature about Dalmatia, which makes it more attractive than traditional sea resorts, where the sand gets into everything.

We found the linen shop and also more of the bed-sheets we wanted, though again not as many as we required. March, in English, asked the lady in the shop if they had more.

'Ah, you must be the English from Povlja!' she exclaimed.

'We thought first you vere Dutch'.

We were amazed that news travelled so fast and so far and wondered what we had done to make it do so! Alas again the stock was thin on the ground and no more sheets were going to be available for some time. Nevertheless we were able to buy other items of crockery and pans we needed. The lady shook us warmly by the hand and we strolled off to explore what else Bol had to offer in the way of shops.

There was a sprinkling of shops along the picturesque high street, including grocers, butchers and an electrical shop plus a couple of banks with a "hole in the wall". Getting cash had not been as easy as we were used to; there was no bank or cash point in Povlja and no cash point in Selca, which did however have a bank where we could get cash over the counter on our Visa card.

This had been a bit of a performance. The transactions involved the production of one's passport, the swiping of the Visa card, an entry made on a computer and the signing of a handwritten form, all in all taking about ten minutes. However the two girls in the bank were charming and we began to enjoy our visits there albeit at first being a little impatient at the slowness. We were going to have to relax and accept the more laid back atmosphere, so what, we had all the time in the world.

Not far from the cash-point there was also a little vegetable market near the harbour. The vegetables available were only those in season but were organic and quite excellent so we stocked up for a few days. In February most of the restaurants and cafes in Bol were closed but we did find a café right on the little harbour wall. In the glorious sunshine it was time to relax and enjoy a beer and watch the little fishing boats coming and going. We then ventured off to find the hardware store on the outskirts of Bol as we were determined to find our cream paint.

'Sorry only white paint, but ve hev colour bottles.' Said the shop assistant and he pointed to some small plastic bottles; there was red, green, brown, yellow and blue. On enquiry I discovered that it was acrylic colouring. With the brown, a light almost sienna colour, I was sure I could mix the white to a sort of cream. It was worth a try anyway!

Back home I gave it a try. Success! With a test mix I was able to make just the cream we wanted so the next day we set about painting in earnest; the wall of the house first and then the terrace walls. We also painted the plaster walls in our bedroom and the living room in the same cream. It wasn't long before Robi and Erika came out to admire our handiwork along with Lijeka our immediate next-door neighbour.

'Werry nice, I like,' said Robi and Erika and Ljeka agreed.

'But you know, not stand werry hot sun.'

'Time will tell,' I said.

The news must have spread quickly because it wasn't long before more than the average number of strollers from the village, taking the sea air out at the Punta, paused to look at our cream walls. One couple said they really liked the cream and asked if we would allow them to use cream on their rendered walls!

I then thought I would do some trompe l'oeil artwork on the outside of the house for added interest. On the new cream wall I painted imitation stonework round both our bedroom and the living room windows in the Austrian style. Above the living room window, as though it was perched on the imitation stonework, I painted a large green lizard similar to one I had seen racing across the road the previous day. I then painted a lemon tree in a large terracotta pot on the porch wall just by our front door with one of the lemons at ground level as though it had fallen. I had noticed that the houses in the village had a lot of lemon trees but ours was lemon tree free, so at least I had rectified that in some way.

Robi's comment was: 'Ah you have lemons all year round!'

'Vat lizard do, vait for fly?' he laughed. That was a good idea so I painted a fat fly within striking distance of the lizard.

The next day Franika called in with Suzy for a chat, quite a normal thing in Povlja, and noticed the lemon tree. She rushed forward to admire it and if by instinct she bent down to try to pick up the fallen painted lemon. She almost immediately realised her mistake and laughed, covering her face in embarrassment and proceeded to chatter away in Croatian in amazement.

Never had I had such interest and adulation for one of my paintings.

'My grandma say lemons look good enough to eat,' said Suzy.

The lizard caused her even more amazement as she recoiled away from it muttering to it as though she was not too sure whether it would bite.

*

We were not happy with our roof. It was ribbed grey asbestos-type sheeting, as indeed a lot of the houses had, though quite a few had those lovely Mediterranean terracotta pantiles. We were not into having the roof redone with the expense of pantiles, so we decided to have it painted in terracotta, as indeed Robi and Erika had, which was a pleasing second best.

We asked around for someone who could do the job as March had forbidden me to go up on the roof. Suzy came up with the name of a painter in the village who did a lot of painting roofs and agreed to bring him along and act as interpreter to size up the job and give us a quote. Dragan the painter and Suzy duly arrived the next day. He was a small wiry, very fit looking little man with a dark tanned wrinkled face, though well into his sixties. I pointed to Robi's roof and also showed him a terracotta pantile I had acquired and explained through Suzy that I wanted our roof exactly that colour. He said that he would do the job for 100DMs(about £33) and he would arrange for the paint to be ordered which we would pay for when we collected it. He said that he would do a priming coat and two coats of the terracotta colour. This was going to be interesting having just had our cream paint experience.

The paint duly arrived a few days later and we went with Dragan to collect and pay for it. We then retired to our house to watch him mix a trial colour; apart from the white acrylic paint he had tubs of red and yellow. The sample pot he mixed and the little bit we painted on a board seemed quite close to what we wanted so we told him to go ahead. Dragan leaped about our roof like one of the Gibraltar apes held by a rope, which was attached to our chimney. The first day he completed the primer coat and on the second day he mixed the terracotta colour and pressed on with the first coat.

We left him to it and went to the shop and had a coffee in our favourite café. When we got back half the roof had been painted. But not a terracotta like the sample. I signalled to Dragan that the colour was not right by a bit of hand signalling and a bit of German of which he had a few words. The colour was too red and clearly needed more yellow or something. We agreed however that he should press on with the colour he had mixed and we would make sure the colour of the third and last coat was right.

The next day, March and I stood over Dragan whilst he mixed the final coat but try as he could it was not right. It was still too red. With just the red and yellow colouring I could not see that were going to achieve what we really wanted, so I produced the small colouring pot I had used for the cream paint. This sienna colour might just be what we needed; it certainly changed the colour to terracotta in a small pot. So we piled into the car and set off for Bol to the paint shop for more of the colouring pots. They only had six so that would have to do, as indeed it did fortunately.

Dragan duly completed the final coat, and though it wasn't 100%, it was near enough and we were happy. We certainly didn't want to carry on mixing colours to achieve perfection. I then gave Dragan the money we had agreed on. He counted it and said in broken German:

'Not enough, I had extra time going to get extra colours.'

'But you agreed to paint our roof terracotta and said you could do it. The extra time was because we had to go to Bol to get the extra colour,' I tried to explain, but he still insisted on more money.

Try as I could in German and sign language I could not get over to him that he had agreed to mix the right colour for the price and that it was his fault that it was not the right colour when he mixed it! He went off on his little scooter muttering.

We mentioned this to Suzy that night and she said she was appalled and would sort it out. Suzy had a very tough side to her so I could imagine that Dragan was going to get a bit of a tongue-lashing.

After that we never heard another peep out of him although he continued to wave to us cheerfully when we saw him. He had obviously thought he could squeeze more cash out of the English. Perhaps he had heard of the extra money we had paid the Man from Imotski. We were beginning to learn the ways of the Balkans and wouldn't be caught again.

Amidst all this painting activity March was busy with her sewing machine making curtains for the living room and curtains with matching bedspreads for the bedrooms. We had bought enough material in Jersey and had somehow managed to squeeze it all in the car. This was fortunate, as we didn't see any curtain material on Brac or in Split; they all seemed to use net curtains. March was frustrated at not being able to "dress" the windows as many people do in Britain.

The windows opened inwards so that the curtains were all hung on poles, which she hated. She duly made the curtains to hang on the poles and although they looked all right to me with the lovely patterns March had chosen, March charged me with the task of thinking up a scheme to eventually put up English tracks and pelmets which would cope with the inward opening windows, particularly as we would have the same problem when we found a house in France. Although I had helped to "dress" our windows in Jersey, this was going to exercise the old grey matter.

Apart from doing the murals I had also managed to find some time to do a little oil painting. The weather had improved a great deal through February so I had set myself up with easel and paints to tackle some of the exquisite scenery. The first picture was of some boats along the harbour wall, looking out to sea with the big grey mountains on the mainland coast in the background.

It could have been the summer; it was quite warm in the sun, and the sky was a lovely brilliant blue with not a cloud to be seen. The sea, as clear as you would see anywhere in the world, was flat calm reflecting not only the blue sky but the boats, the trees on the headland and the mountains. I was frantic to get down on the canvass this tranquil and colourful scene.

What we hadn't been prepared for though was the amazing sunsets which we started to get. I tried hard to get down the riots of colour onto the canvass, but the colours changed so quickly and dramatically that I resorted to taking photographs and making quick watercolour sketches before I started a canvass. The views from our terrace both during the day and evening sunset were stunning. We not only had the coast stretching to the west towards Split but a five mile stretch of sea across to the mainland with its tall rugged mountain range stretching away as far as the eye could see to the north and south. What intrigued me was how the grey limestone mountains changed colour so much with the varying weather. Sometimes brilliant white, sometimes cream, and once in a thunderstorm in the early evening they were a dark blue like the sea and sky. At sunset they reflected the bright colours going from apricot to a dark magenta in the last moments before the sun went down. There were so many permutations of scenes I could paint I knew I had plenty to keep my leisure time filled; who knows I might even sell some one day!!

However, I soon used up the handful of canvasses I had brought from Jersey. Where was I going to find an art supplier on Brac?

'You hev to go to Split' said Robi, which was predictable.

Before we managed to get away to Split I decided in the absence of canvasses to paint a picture on our living room wall with a trompe l'oeil frame to make it stand out from the wall. I was pleased with the effect particularly as it fooled one or two of our friends who were always popping in; they were always trying to straighten the frame which I had painted a little askew.

We duly set off for Split, early as we also wanted to explore the large vegetable market there and the rest of the city we hadn't seen before; but you also have to keep reminding yourself that the shops shut at midday sharp and do not open again until 4.30 or 5pm. We found an art shop in one of the little narrow streets near to the ruins of Diocletian's palace but alas the only canvasses were not much bigger than a postage stamp; this was no good for me as I liked to use quite large sizes.

'Will you be getting in any more larger sizes soon,' I asked the lady who spoke good English.

'Only if I make more money, then I can order some more.' She said sadly.

She did however say that there was another art shop and drew us a sketch of how to get there. We sauntered through the narrow streets, which were paved in large slabs of stone. These had become highly polished by the millions of feet, which had walked on them over the centuries, so much so that they glistened like a street of marble after a recent rainfall. The houses and shops showed the Italian and Venetian influence making you feel that you were in Florence or Sorrento. The shops were smart though many were closed in the winter.

Eventually we emerged from the old city into the modern part with its austere concrete and glass buildings in the old communist style. We found the art shop in a concrete tiered monstrosity, which was reminiscent of a German concrete bunker from World War 2. This large shopping mall had a good selection of shops but we noticed that many of the available shops to let were empty. The art shop to my great delight was well stocked so I bought as many canvasses as we could carry. Our trip to the market on our way back was also productive as it was well stocked with a much bigger selection vegetables than we had found on the island. This also explained the large number of islanders we had seen on the ferries, loaded down with bags full of vegetables. We caught a ferry back to the island in time to have lunch in a little restaurant on the harbour in Supetar. We sat next to the large open wood fire and ordered fish and some Dalmatian white wine. The name of the fish was quite unpronounceable but it was deliciously cooked with herbs, and the white wine the waiter had recommended made us feel that we were at last having more good days than bad or frustrating ones.

'Perhaps we should delay our decision to sell the house and get out,' said March.

I nodded thoughtfully but nevertheless feeling that we really had found something special.

MAGIC LANTERN SHOW!

Chapter 6

The Bura

The weather towards the end of February and early March was beginning to get noticeably warmer and most days were sunny, so much so that we were eating our three meals every day on our terrace overlooking the sea. The snow was also beginning to disappear on the mountains along the mainland coast and the sea was calm reflecting the clear blue sky with hardly a cloud in sight.

The stretch of sea between the Island and the mainland remained quiet. But occasionally we had seen the odd tramp steamer passing between us and the mainland and often some large fishing boats heading south towards Dubrovnik, but mostly the sea remained devoid of any activity, though with the warmer weather and calmer seas we were now getting a few of the locals putting out in their little boats. These were wooden mainly and solidly built, though there was a smattering of fibreglass ones. These little boats were well cared for and all newly painted, white of course, but sometimes with a coloured stripe along the side. I had included several of these boats in my paintings of the harbour riding on their moorings stern to the harbour wall and bow onto an anchorage angled towards the open sea. Below the boats the water in the harbour was so clear that the stones on the seabed could be clearly seen with the boats casting a shadow on them; this had been quite a challenge to paint but an enjoyable one.

One thing we noticed sitting on our terrace was the lack of seagulls. We never saw more than two at any one time and became convinced that this was the only pair in Povlja, so we of course called them Mr and Mrs Seagull. In Jersey there were hundreds of seagulls everywhere, not just along the coast, out to sea, and in the harbours, but in the town of St Helier where they were becoming a nuisance. They had been fed so much by the tourists and some of the locals that they lost the skill of finding their traditional food. Their numbers had grown and they were all big and fat and greedy; a bit like some of the bankers in Jersey. They raided rubbish bags and stole food from tables and in some cases snatched food from your hands. Eventually it became illegal to feed them, though some misguided idiots continued to do so.

Mr and Mrs Seagull in Povlja were quite different though. They were herring gulls like the ones in Jersey, but they were leaner and fitter looking; a bit like the Dalmatian local human population. We never saw them anywhere near our local bins and nobody fed them, so they obviously retained their natural skills for catching fish, though occasionally you would see them following some of the fishing boats as they came into the harbour. However, they wouldn't get much from the fishermen as just about everything was eaten and the rest given to the cats of which there were many around the village.

All the stray cats were fed by our neighbour Lijeka, who seemed to collect them, having between eight or nine around at any one time. We obviously had no worries about mice but on the other hand Rupert hated cats and was continually trying to get at them. We had trained Rupert from being a puppy to chase cats as we were fed up with neighbours cats in Jersey messing in our garden and on our terrace; the cats were also killing some of the bird life. Rupert was quite good at it and soon had the local cats out of the garden. Being in Povlja with all Lijeka's strays must have seemed like home to him. He certainly did a lot of chasing about when he saw one, and this was then followed by peeing on all the strategic points of his territory, with great aplomb!

That night we woke up to hear a noise. It was about two o'clock in the morning and somewhere outside we heard engine noises and what seemed to be voices.

'There's someone out there,' said March in a hushed whisper.

March armed herself with a broom and I grabbed my old Gurkha kukri.

Stealthily, in the best military tradition, I opened the bedroom shutters and window, which overlooked the sea and we both peered out into the darkness. It was pitch black outside and our eyes were struggling to get used to the dark. I instructed March to open her mouth and look out of the corner of her eyes, in the best military tradition of fieldcraft.

We did not have street lights out at the Punta. But as our eyes acclimatised, we saw not too far out to sea some lights shining on the water and heard voices jabbering away. Being a still night the voices carried as though they were just in front of the house. If I spoke Croatian I would have understood quite clearly what they were saying. It was obviously a few local fishing boats hauling in their catches because we could eventually make out the fishermen in the glow of the lights, which looked like large Victorian lampshades directing the light into the water. We later found out that they were gas lamps, which were used to attract the fish and squid.

*

One early sunny March day, whilst sitting on the terrace having tea with Erica we heard what appeared to be a ferocious dogfight nearby. I immediately got up to look for Rupert but was sure he could not be involved as the stonewalls of the garden were four foot high. However, one of the dogs did sound very like a ferocious Rupert at his worst. He had been in one or two fights on the beach in Jersey so I knew what an angry Rupert sounded like. I shot round to Erika and Robi's house from where the noise seemed to be emanating.

Sure enough there was Rupert and Ruff, Robi's large Alsatian, engaged in combat with Robi trying hard to intervene. I grabbed Rupert's collar and Robi did the same to Ruff. I was concerned that Rupert was injured as Ruff had bitten him but he had given as good as he had got, however, it was lucky Robi and I were there so quickly because Ruff was a big dog. We shoved the dogs in our respective houses and Robi and I joined the girls for tea.

Robi was amazed at Rupert. 'Ven I first see your dog, I tort pretty little English lapdog, but today he fights like lion!'

The event was quite unexpected as Rupert and Ruff had met in our garden on several occasions and seemed to be all right with one another. However, not long before the fight Ruff had been servicing a bitch from the village, so Rupert must have got wind of it and decided to move in on the act.

It was on this occasion that we were reminded by Erika and Robi, that the last three strong Buras of the winter occurred on the 7th, 17th and 27th of March.

'De Bura, you know, alvays come dees days,' said Robi knowingly.

We were most amused by this. How could this be so accurate and regular every year?

On the 7th we awoke to a lovely sunny day with a flat calm sea and no wind. Robi and Erika's shutters were already closed.

'They really believe this Bura timing,' I said to March.

We pottered around in the garden for most of the morning but then realised that we had no bread for lunch so decided to nip into the village in the car as it was almost midday. As we were getting the car out of the garage, which was below the house, Lijeka came along pointing out to sea and in the general direction of the gap in the mountains on the mainland coast; an earthquake had apparently caused this gap about a hundred years before.

'Bura, Bura', she exclaimed.

We peered out to sea but could not see anything and certainly no change in the weather, so we were beginning to wonder whether Lijeka was going off her head. We then saw, below the gap in the mountains, a slightly darker sea close to the mainland and in it was a faint line of white horses.

'Lets nip into the village and quickly pick up our bread before the shop closes. We will close everything up when we get back', I said confidently.

In the village shop we saw Suzy and told her what we had just seen.

'Of course it's the 7th March. Bura always come today', she said, but she didn't dash off as her house was tucked into the lea of the hill and not really affected by the Bura.

By the time we drove along the harbour and reached the brow of the hill at the Punta, we had taken only five minutes on the round trip, the sea was a mass of large waves and white horses. The car was buffeted as we drove the last two hundred yards to our house. We found the garage doors banging in the wind, so had to hold them back with a couple of large stones, to get the car into the garage. Walking, or rather struggling back to the house, we held on to one another and leant into the wind. We rushed inside to close the shutters on the seaward side. The wind was already howling in the gutters but the sun shone brightly as indeed it did during most Buras.

'Who would have thought that it would have blown up so quickly!' said March.

'We will have to keep an eye on Robi's and Erika's shutters in future.'

The Bura raged on into the evening and with it came the inevitable power cut right in the middle of a John Wayne film on Croatian TV. It was time to go to bed by candlelight and do some reading. We felt rather cosy and safe in our warm bed and mellow candle light with our little strong stone house protecting us from the raging Bura outside. We dozed off to the howling wind and the crashing noise of the waves breaking on the stone beach. At two in the morning I awoke to complete silence, the Bura had gone. I did, however, have to get up and turn off all the house lights now that we had power again.

Waking up, or sometimes being woken up by one thing or another, was becoming a habit in Povlja. We also always woke up together in some sort of sympathetic awakening.

Our immediate drill was that one of us would make some tea (very English) and we would sit up in bed, chatting or reading, sipping our tea and munching delicious Croatian biscuits, until we dozed off again.

One night we were sipping our tea with just March's bedside light on, and by chance I moved my arm above my head and cast a shadow on the bedroom wall over on my side. I immediately remembered my father using his hands to cast shadows of birds and animals on the wall to amuse my sister and me at bedtime when we were small children. I decided to have a go much to the amusement of March who also joined in. We certainly became quite good at birds and animals, particularly snakes and crocodiles, which were easy, but then attempted peoples heads. I remembered my father did a good silhouette of Ghandi, whose features he had no doubt memorised as a result of his five war-years in India. I very nearly managed to do a Ghandi, but I was more successful with General de Gaulle.

' Watch this one!' I said and held my thumb up above my private parts so that it cast a shadow like a large penis.

'Stop boasting,' exclaimed March. This made us go into fits of laughter as it was so much fun and often became a feature of our night-time insomnia. Or was it post Bura stress disorder.

Occasionally when we awoke in the middle of the night, we would switch on the television onto the only channel open after midnight to find to our delight that they were running episodes of 'Allo, Allo',' Blackadder' or 'Fawlty Towers'; we once watched the whole series of 'Fawlty Towers' over the course of four nights; quite a treat even without the sound. What amazed us was that the Croatians loved all these British comedy series and even understood some of the more subtle and bizarre aspects of our humour. We certainly could not imagine some of the western European nations understanding and enjoying our humour.

Our Saturday visits to Robi and Erika's Pizzeria continued well into March. Sitting around the log fire eating our pizzas and sipping our local red wine we got to know many of their young friends from the village. They all spoke English and were intensely interested in what England (they always referred to England and never Britain) was like, and how we did things. Although Tito had been a good and benign dictator, Yugoslavia had been isolated from the West and had been under communism for over half a century. They had also suffered under the corrupt regime of President Tudjman for over ten years. That regime was now over and following democratic elections they now had a democratic government and a democratically elected president who had little real power, quite unlike his predecessors. We asked how the new government was doing but nobody was prepared to commit themselves after only just over a year in power. At this time the government had done nothing concrete to make substantial changes to how things were run, but to be fair it was early stages.

'A lot of promises, but no action yet!' said one of their friends.

They were all basically sceptical in that those who had been elected were still the old communists under a different guise with not a great deal of new blood infused into the government. This applied to all levels of government right down to the local commune, where the old and bold were still in power.

'All they have done is changed their suits!' one of them chimed in.

Their main grudge was that the older generations still held the power and young people did not get a look in. There were many changes they wanted to make locally but they knew they would not be accepted, or even given a hearing, until the older generation had passed on. We suggested that one of them or more should stand in the local elections but they all seemed to have this strange negative resignation to the fact that they would never succeed and that if they did they would be fighting a losing battle against the older members on the council who did not want change.

'Why don't you start a pressure group amongst the younger ones and insist on the changes you want,' queried March. 'Then perhaps one of you might eventually get elected,' she continued.

'They will shut us out,' one of them replied.

One problem in Croatia, due to their isolation under communism, was what to change to. They now had democracy in name, but they didn't know what it was. The situation was a blank page on which they had no real idea of what to write.

As well intentioned as some of the new politicians in central government were, how could they introduce reforms with no knowledge of how to run a democracy, or how to introduce a market driven economy. What the country badly needed was this expertise. They needed many of the Croatians, who had emigrated and had been successful, to return to Croatia to enter public life. (Croatia has more of their people living abroad than in Croatia). But would the present people in power make room for them; doubtful.

One thing about these interesting discussions was that it made us appreciate our own democracy, which had taken centuries to mature and was the envy of the world, and made us feel proud of what our nation had achieved. We had the feeling that it was going to take more than this young generation of Croatians to make the necessary changes.

*

On one of our morning trips to the village we bumped into the Dutch couple and over a cup of coffee on the quayside we heard of their latest problems in setting up a water sports centre out at the Punta. They seemed to be getting nowhere with the local bureaucracy tying them up with paperwork and delays, plus opposition from certain people who also had vested interests in the Punta as an area for development.

Because of this delay they were putting one of their other plans into operation, to open a restaurant on the quay. They had leased the old olive pressing building and were having the old presses removed and had already engaged a builder following the approval of their plans. The village were behind them on this development as they needed a smart restaurant by the harbour to attract the tourists, so this was proceeding fairly smoothly. They were also going to open an ice cream parlour and a bar further along the quay.

This all seemed to be admirable and they were full of talk for their plans, but something didn't seem quite right to us. They didn't seem to be the sort of people with money; they talked of another partner but we felt he was probably more likely their backer.

We wished them well with their plans but decided

to reserve our bets on whether they were going to be a success. The one thing the village didn't need was foreigners coming in with grandiose plans, getting the backing of the people, and then the whole thing ending in a disaster. Croatia needed investment to get tourism going, but we hoped that the Dutch, as everyone called them, were going to get it right.

The weather in March continued to improve considerably. Every day, getting longer, was sunny and warm though we were not tempted to swim in the sea as our friends said it would still be too cold. Mind you we were used to sea temperatures of only 16C in Jersey so we were perhaps getting soft. We were still eating our three meals a day on our terrace looking out across the clear blue sea. The "horrors" of January seemed a long time gone and we were enjoying ourselves. We decided to do some walking and started to explore the outer limits of the village and the surrounding olive groves.

Behind our house the land was terraced up to the top of the hill with numerous stone walls enclosing what had been the old vineyards from pre 1920 days, before the wine industry had been devastated. Some had been filled with olive trees but many were grown over with scrub and small bushy fir trees. We discovered a back way to the village winding up through terraces, some of which had smart stone houses on them, about the same vintages as ours, but others had half finished structures. These had been started during the tourist boom before the Balkan war of the early 1990s but when tourism was destroyed by the war and money ran out, the houses were never finished. One of the houses previously owned by a Serb and almost finished was up for sale, we were told, for DM 24,000 (about £8,000). The Serb could never return after the war so it was going cheaply. A tempting investment if one was able to get all the paperwork organised through Serbia.

We were pretty sure the tourist boom would return to Croatia once the western presumption that it was still a war zone had been dispelled. (Our friends in Jersey were still referring to Croatia as a war zone). There were certainly signs that tourism was reviving, if a little slowly. There were many opportunities to buy holiday homes here quite cheaply now that restrictions on foreigners buying had been relaxed.

The half finished houses gave an interesting insight into how their houses were constructed. The bases were solid concrete plinths, with reinforced concrete pillars to form a framework for the hollow brick walls. On top of this the houses were capped with reinforced concrete, which formed a base for either wooden truss roofs, or reinforced concrete pitch roofs. The outside of the houses were faced in substantial Brac stone and the windows lined with smart polished stone. The roofs were either finished in terracotta tiles or corrugated asbestos (or the modern equivalent) and the windows were mostly wooden framed with integral shutters.

In Brac, except for the houses left unfinished from their war, the houses were generally all finished and looked very smart. This was a striking contrast to the houses in most parts of the Balkans where houses were deliberately not finished to avoid paying taxes.

In Bosnia and Herzegovina this was particularly noticeable where we saw very few houses which had been finished. The lack of finish generally meant no rendering or stone finish on the outer walls, with the bare concrete and red brick showing, and no pitch roof. The houses would mostly have a concrete slab at the top of the house with reinforcing rods sticking up like antennas where the roof should be. In the much visited resort of Medjugorje, a Herzegovinan Lourdes, where some children saw a vision of the Virgin Mary, very few of the houses were finished and indeed most of it looked like a shanty town; not uncommon with many towns in the Balkans. I suppose when you are too poor to pay the tax, or too mean, that is the result. Happily this does not apply to Brac or the Dalmatian coast where the houses are smart and well finished, often in an Italian/Venetian style, and all well cared for.

*

Buying a house, now that restrictions on foreigners have been lifted, can vary in complexity. Ours was reasonably simple as it was a comparatively new house with only one previous owner. We passed contract, paid the money, had the transaction recorded by the town hall and our name put in the "Book of Land". Final approval still had to be given by the Croatian Foreign Office in Zagreb and this, we were told, took anything from six months to two years. The "Book of Land" is most important as we had heard many stories where contracts had been exchanged but the all important entry had not been made. One case we heard of was in Herzegovina, where it was discovered by the owner of a house, that his name was not in the "Book of Land", but that of a Turk who died over 200 years ago.

Where the houses are much older, like France, it may take some time to complete, often because when the owner has died, all the relatives have to be contacted to give their permission. If the house is Serb owned there is the difficulty of communications with Serbia and arranging the purchase. With much older houses there may also be problems over the exact boundaries of the property. House purchase is a pretty fraught business anywhere, particularly in the UK, but we certainly found it very easy in Croatia.

We were not the only foreigners to have bought in Povlja. There was a German couple in the village, who were living their permanently, and a retired Austrian couple who had built a house two plots from us, as a holiday home. We had also heard much to everyone's interest that an American had bought a plot of land next to the Austrians and intended to build a house quite soon. The village was beginning to have an international flavour.

As we continued on our walk, we looked down towards the sea and spotted a small inlet with a little harbour containing just two little fishing boats. On the other side of the inlet, right on the water's edge, was a delightful house with a little boat moored at the foot of some steps. It was a location to die for, but we later learned that the house had been built illegally without any planning permission, and as a result had no mains water, electricity or mains sewage. It was well built and was a house of character, but the authorities had ordered the old man who had built it to pull it down. However, for twenty years he had staunchly refused and was still clinging to his property. He obviously had friends in high places.

We continued to the outskirts of the village where the church and old Roman fort overlook the harbour and wandered through the little old streets where the old stone houses also had thick slabs of stone as roof tiles, often cemented together and painted white(of course). Several steep sets of steps connected the upper village to the houses around the harbour and we descended down one set of these to a welcome beer in a café on the quay; the end to a perfect leisurely walk. We would have to that again.

We were getting much more organised with our shopping for food. Our local shop was a bit limited in its stock but we had discovered a shop in Selca (which Erika called the metropolis) about ten minutes away. There were three grocers shops, a large one and two small ones. The small ones were not much larger than our living room and the larger ones they called supermarkets were like a local village store in the UK.

We tried all three but decided to shop regularly at the one next to the church because it seemed to cram more interesting stock into its small space than all the rest put together. It was rather like the little shops I remembered from my boyhood in the Yorkshire Dales. There was not much room to move and because everything was crowded together you were in danger of missing something. However, the chap who ran it spoke good English and was keen to help us do our shopping. He was tall, bearded and very friendly and rushed about the shop to find what we wanted including diving into their back store for things. He was a bit like young Granville in Arkwright's store in "Open all Hours", though not in looks. His business partner was at the little cash desk by the door. She was an attractive blonde who spoke no English but was again very friendly. It was a real pleasure to shop there.

We always had to remember to get to Selca well before eleven in the morning so that we could catch the butcher. We had noted that none of the butchers in Selca, Bol or Supetar spoke English; probably some sort of qualification. However, we knew we could always resort to animal impersonations, at least March could, as I would generally pretend not to be with her if she started. I had decided to learn the names for pork, lamb and beef but the problem was that they never seemed to understand my Croatian pronunciation. Anyway March was always hovering at my shoulder with the odd snort.

We also had to remember to take our empty wine bottles back to the shop otherwise we would be charged for the bottle; our garage, filled with empty bottles, is testimony to our forgetfulness.

Vegetable shopping was still hit and miss in both Povlja and Selca as we relied upon the travelling vans who never seemed to keep to the same days. Some days there would be two or three on the square in Selca and other days none at all. Occasionally they would turn up on the quay in Povlja in the evenings when the local shop opened at five pm. We therefore often went off to Bol or Supetar where there were morning markets every day. It was also a chance to fill up with petrol as these were the only two places on the island with fuel stations.

Chapter 7

No Problem

As the month drew on we enjoyed the sunshine and even the Buras, which turned up on cue, but we were now anxious to get to France to find a house. We were told that the Spring is when new houses tended to come on the market so we had to move on. This we were now reluctant to do as we were really happy there. The weather was gorgeous, our little house was smart, refurbished and furnished and we had made some really good friends. It was also a painter's paradise and I was pleased with my paintings. Our initial troubles were almost forgotten and indeed we had decided to postpone our original 'knee jerk' reaction that we had made a hideous mistake and we should do the place up and sell it.

We had one or two loose ends to tie up. The man from the water company had turned up to read the meter and we had paid him in cash as was the norm, but we still had to pay for the electricity. Most of the villagers did this through the post office having faxed their meter readings on the post office fax. The electricity company then faxed back the amount they owed and they then paid the bill at the post office.

However we needed to go to the electricity company offices in Supetar to check that the 'Man from Imotski' had given them the correct meter readings when he left and that our name was recorded as the new account holders. We therefore set off for Supetar and eventually found the electricity company offices in a back street of a housing estate. Armed with our meter readings from arrival to those we had just noted down, we were directed to an office upstairs where a pleasant English speaking lady looked up the account on the computer. Not only did we then have to produce our passports but we had to produce the house deeds and contract of sale. We were quite amused by this.

'As if we would turn up to pay someone else's bill!' said March.

The bill was sorted out and we went down to the cashier's desk downstairs to pay, only having again, to our amazement, to show all the documents again.

After this amusing experience we went down to the harbour in Supetar where the vegetable market was located as we needed fruit for the journey to France. We went to our usual stall where a young friendly woman who spoke very good English always served us. She was tall and on the large side with blonde hair, looking much more Germanic than Croatian.

However, that is not too unusual in Croatia, which was

under the Austro-Hungarian Empire for a long time. The telephone book in Zagreb and the names on the graves there testify to the long period of Austrian influence. We busily examined the fruit with what we assumed to be girl's grandfather hovering in close attention offering a variety of other things we did not want. This had always been a feature at her stall. A few sharp words from her however, always called off her grandfather, who then always looked suitably hurt and retired to the back of the stall. We usually got a smile and a wink after she had done this.

As we were about to leave the stall, a smart, expensively dressed middle aged woman, who had also been buying there, asked us if we spoke German. She had that forthrightness of a German, and her manner was such that I almost sprang to attention and clicked my heals. I replied that I did and she then asked us if we wanted to buy a house.

' We already had a house in Povlja,' I replied.

She then exclaimed that: 'Supetar is much nicer than Povlja. So much more to do and see.'

She said this as though it was a fact caste in concrete; there was no argument.

I humbly said that I didn't agree and whilst we liked Supetar, we were quite happy where we were. This did not deter her as she went on to describe her house in detail. It was large with two garages, a big garden and a view of the sea from the top of the hill behind the town. We started to walk towards where we had parked the car saying that we were not interested but she continued on her sales pitch. It turned out that she was a Croatian who spoke fluent German and said she did not need such a big house anymore. She was selling at DM 180,000 (about £60,000), which was an excellent price if all she said about it was true.

Eventually we broke free saying we hoped she found a buyer and shot off quickly, just in case she started at us again, to hide in a café on the other side of the harbour to have a refreshing Croatian beer.

We had decided to leave on 30th March and to drive to France via Zagreb, Slovenia, Austria and southern Germany. We planned to stop in Zagreb to visit my son and his wife and my little grand daughter. Basically, this was the route we came into Croatia in January. However, first we had to shut up the house and say fond farewells to our friends. They all wanted to know when we would be back but we were unable to say, as we had no idea how soon we would find a house in France. Robi and Erica volunteered to keep a key and look after the house whilst we were away. In fact, quite a lot of our friends said they would keep an eye on the house. Eventually we tore ourselves away and drove up the winding road out of the village to the top of the hill where we caught a last glimpse of the picturesque harbour and village. We really didn't want to leave and the memory of Erica with tears in her eyes remained with us.

After the ferry to Split we drove up through the majestic Dinaric Alps and through the deserted countryside, which March still insisted on calling "bandit country" and back through the town of Knin, which looks such an inhospitable place compared with the Dalmatian coast. We couldn't get through this area quickly enough for March who sat very tensed up clutching our dog Rupert. Fortunately it wasn't too long before we arrived at the Plitvicka National Park and much more attractive scenery.

It took about seven hours all told to get to Zagreb where we met my son who had booked us into an hotel, near the centre of the city. It was frequently used by the diplomatic corps and various international organisations, which had proliferated in Zagreb since the war. The hotel had secure parking and was on one of the many tram routes into the city centre which had few parking facilities so trams were the main means of getting about in the city. I have always loved trams, believing them to be the answer to a lot of our inner city traffic problems, so I was looking forward to our first trip. However it was getting late so we had dinner and off to bed in our smart bedroom.

On waking in the morning I reached out to my bedside table for the glass of orange I had left there, only to feel a strange sensation on my hand. Quickly turning on the lamp, as the daylight was still weakly trying to come through the curtains, I saw thousands of ants crawling all over my hand, the bedside table, my glass of orange and the lamp. I leaped out of bed and switched on March's lamp and found the same ant army. Waking March gently I pointed out our little problem.

'What the hell…….!' March shuddered and uttered a few unladylike oaths, very unusual for her, but nevertheless appropriate for the occasion. March, at the best of times hates being awakened prematurely, but this time she was really ticking. We showered and dressed and quickly went along to reception to seek out the manager.

In reception was a large forty year old, rather brash Croatian, who obviously spent a lot on his hair and appearance in general, right down to the bracelets and large rings and his pin-striped suit. He was definitely the man about town; confident, loud and very conscious of his position as the hotel manager. When I told him about the ants he exclaimed in a loud voice, 'No Problem!' and stormed off down the corridor to our room with us in close pursuit.

On seeing the ants he kept a calm and confident air and said again: 'No problem! I vill get girl to psst psst, no problem'. Making a gesture as if holding a spray can.

However, March was having none of this, she was in full dealing with foreigners mode.

'No psst psst ', she said confrontationally.

'This will not be solved with psst psst. We want a new room or we will move out'.

The manager had met his match.

'No problem, I find new room', he said magnanimously.

'You go hev breakfast and we move things to new room.'

So off we went for breakfast, which was near to reception in a clean colourfully decorated restaurant. It was basically a continental style breakfast, which was fine for us; the English breakfast, much as we often yearned for bacon and eggs, had sadly become a rare treat in the interests of our health and waistlines. My coffee and March's hot chocolate were both very good and we tucked into the bread. Not the standard of French bread, but who's is, but nevertheless fresh and wholesome.

On the table were baskets of small butter packs and small foil containers of jams, pastes and honey; this is something we have always hated in hotels. Why can't they make more effort to serve it all fresh in dishes, but then this is the MacDonald's era of pre packed food.

It was then that we noticed that one or two of the foil containers of jam were holed at the top. On closer examination the holes were not caused by thumbnails or the like, but were definitely made by some rodent, with teeth marks in evidence.

We called the waiter who looked suitably horrified and disappeared saying: 'I fetch manager'.

'This will be interesting', said March.

The manager duly arrived and looked suitably mortified when he saw the gnawed packets.

'No problem, wery sorry, ve change', he said, his confidence only slightly dented. We had new jams and for the rest of the meal he hovered about asking if everything was all right.

Breakfast over we resolved to explore Zagreb before lunch. We knew that all the trams on this route would take us into the centre so we duly hopped on one having bought our tickets from a machine at the tram stop. The tram was quite old, though there were some new ones around, and looked very like the trams on the old World War 2 films in many of the central European cities such as the Vienna of "The Third Man". I could almost imagine being in disguise and fleeing the attentions of the Gestapo.

The tram was crowded, as indeed they all were, so we had to stand and hang on to the straps as the tram lurched from both sudden acceleration and deceleration. The trams were all packed and we saw very few cars on the road. It was only a few minutes to the centre where we alighted at the main square, which was a turmoil of trams and people. The square was quite large with the tram stops on one side and shops and cafes all around the other sides.

It was dominated by a large bronze statue of a warrior, waving a sword, on a horse and the whole square swarmed with people dashing about. We noticed that they were either very expensively dressed or looked very poor. We also noticed that rich or poor they nearly all had mobile phones; this craze had certainly hit Croatia in a big way.

Picking our way through the throng towards a large covered market, there suddenly we were confronted with the four Peruvians from "The Fast Show", in their ponchos, large hats, and cowboy boots, playing their strange pipe music and stamping one foot. They were attracting quite a crowd and were doing well selling their tapes and CDs of their music.

The covered market was full of vegetables, fruit, meat and cheese stalls with produce from all over the world. After three months with a very limited selection we feasted our eyes on everything. It was a great shame that we were not buying! We also wandered around quite a lot of the streets, which were mostly pedestrian precincts and noticed that the shops were of high quality with many well-known names represented. Items were expensive by Croatian standards and with thirty percent of the workforce out of work and the average wage on two hundred pounds a month, we wondered who was buying. There were obviously some Croatians who had plenty of money. There was also of course the international community there in abundance with plenty of money.

We then discovered an art shop with the most attractive but unusual paintings in the window. On enquiring we found that the were painted on glass (on the reverse) in oils and the style was called "naïve art". The glass gave them a depth and luminescence, which I had never seen before. The figures and the landscapes were in simple styles, hence "naïve", showing peasants in traditional costumes around their crude dwellings. Many of the scenes were in the snow or at night and the light effects created on the glass were quite stunning. I was sure that this had taken a lot of training and practice, particularly having to paint "back to front", but I was determined to have a go at some time.

We tore ourselves away from these lovely pictures and strolled past the lovely gothic cathedral, through streets lined with tempting cafes and restaurants, up to the top of the hill overlooking the city. Here, the government offices are located near to St Mark's Church where my grand daughter was christened. The buildings were reminiscent of many in all the central European cities and showed the Austrian influence. We found the café we had arranged to meet my son and his family and settled down to a well-deserved Croatian beer from Karlovac.

Lunch was in a delightful little restaurant overlooking the city. The cuisine was Austro-Hungarian in style and quantity. I had a large meal, which was a local dish similar to the Austrian "Bauernschmaus", a dish of sauerkraut covered in various meats and sausages, topped with a large knoedel or dumpling. I had a pretty good attempt at demolishing this but I didn't have the central European capacity for such a large helping, though I could name a few friends who would have done it justice. Fortunately we had a lot more walking and sightseeing to do to walk it all off. One thing we again noticed was that Zagreb, like the Dalmatian coast was a great café society. The place was full of bars, cafes and restaurants where people sat and watched the world go by. Often we would see people eating their own food in the café/bars rather like they do in many places in France; a custom quite alien to us.

We had arranged to meet an old school friend of mine for a beer in a café in the main square at about four o'clock. Whilst we sat and waited for him we noticed again how tall and pretty many of the women were. They had also followed the current western European fashion of wearing a great deal of black clothing and they all seemed to have long black hair.

My friend then popped up at our table. Whilst I had made a career in the British Army having been commissioned from Sandhurst, he had gone to work in America, joined the American Marines and taken American citizenship. He had retired from the US Marine Corps and he was now finding work with various international organisations, mainly the UN, around the world. It was this that had brought him to Croatia during the Balkan war. It was my son who had met him whilst they were both working in Zagreb, showing what a small world it really was now.

It was super to see him again after many years of just sending Christmas cards. He had been a staunch bachelor in the army but had now married a young Croatian girl and had two small children. I was pleased for him that he had a family at last but was glad that my own family had grown up; I was past the nappy and screaming kids stage, content just to have my grandchildren for short periods. We agreed to stay in closer contact now that we had the Croatian link.

When we got back to the hotel we found our new room, smaller than the first, but still comfortable. However our bedside lights did not work! In fact there was quite a lot of wiring hanging out of the skirting board. Then March closed the curtains and the whole pole came down, curtains and all. I called the manager on the house phone and he appeared with the maintenance man and his girlfriend, saying:

'No problem, we fix'.

The room was not big, but with five of us in there it seemed as though we were squashed into a broom cupboard. The lights were fixed, but the wires still hung out of the wall.

'No problem, but don't touch', ordered the manager.

Pointing to the cable March demanded another room but none was available. The girlfriend and maintenance man, suitably supervised by the manager put back the curtains.

'No problem', said the manager as they all trooped out. We had to laugh, this was Croatian Fawlty Towers at its best. We wondered whether he cuffed the waiter like Basil Fawlty. Having had a light meal before we left the city centre, and being exhausted after a busy day, we retired to bed to watch TV and dozed off to sleep hoping that the ants did not find us or the exposed cables did not catch fire!

Next morning, thankfully ant free, we trooped off to breakfast. However, breakfast was not rodent free as there were several foil containers of jam nibbled by some little pest. When the manager arrived, for the first time a crack was appearing in his confident exterior. His face fell and for a change he found that "no problem" was not the right thing to say, having seen the look on March's face.

'I werry sorry, I get new ones,' he said sheepishly.

March had spent over twenty years in hotel management, so I usually left this sort of situation to her. One look from her was more than a match for over confident, macho hotel managers. Everything was changed but it was time to go. We had arranged with the receptionist the night before to make up our bill as I wanted to make sure we had enough cash (he had insisted on cash). However, the Manager could not find the bill.

'Agh, these Balkans', he exclaimed, referring to the receptionist.

Regaining his confidence, he said, 'No problem, I make new one'.

His comment about the "Balkans" intrigued us as the receptionist had been very helpful and had seemed quite efficient and intelligent girl.

Anyway we thought we were in the Balkans.

Soon we were driving on our way through the cobbled streets towards the outskirts of the city, trying to avoid being stuck in the tramlines. I remembered back in the nineteen sixties, whilst stationed in Germany, that my little Volkswagen Beetle had often been stuck in the tramlines which seem to have been set deep in the cobbled streets and only a sharp turn on the steering wheel would get you out of trouble. Zagreb is not far from the Slovenian border so we were soon winging our way through changing scenery, in particular we were climbing into hilly country which soon revealed the mountains. The architecture also changed to Tyrolean-style houses and farms. It wasn't long before we were onto a motorway and speeding past the Slovenian capital of Ljubljana. The motorway then took us towards the Austrian town of Villach, just over the border.

When we got to the border we noticed quite a number of Austrian border guards in military fatigues. Our passports were checked by a friendly girl, who waved us on, but then before we could drive more than a few yards, a young official leaped out of the crowd of officials and motioned us to pull to the side. He asked us if we had anything to declare and when we said no, he asked us to open the rear door of our estate and to offload everything onto benches at the side of the lay-by.

As we offloaded piece by piece he became more and more dejected at not finding anything. After my paintings, paints and easel, there was March's sewing machine, her fabric art pictures, material and wools and silks. When we half unloaded he said desperately, 'Ok, we look in the roof', referring to the box or Thule on the roof rack.

'No, we will finish offloading the car for you,' March insisted.

In the Thule we had most of our clothing, including all our ski gear, in plastic bags. By now he had had enough as all this had taken about half an hour with our heavily laden car. We speculated that he must have been suspicious of a Luxembourg registered car (an interim measure until we found a house in France), heavily laden, British passports, but living in Croatia.

We had almost finished reloading when he returned with new hope.

'Let me see dog's papers', he said curtly.. These we duly handed over in a smart folder, which contained his vaccination record, certificate of rabies vaccination and his electronic chip details.

'I don't recognise any of these signatures', he said looking at the vaccination records.

By now I was a bit annoyed. 'Of course you won't ', I said, 'They are signatures of vets in Jersey.'

He muttered about getting their customs vet to

examine Rupert, but I pressed on getting more annoyed.

'Are you telling me you don't recognise British vets?' I replied.

He thought for a moment, closed the documents and handed them back to me.

'You may go', he said rather reluctantly and walked off in a huff.

We packed, "double quick", and drove off with all the customs people staring at us.

'Get a move on, before they change their minds', muttered March.

We were soon clear and driving at speed through the glorious Austrian scenery. We speculated on why there were so many customs officials at the border and concluded that it was probably because Slovenia then was not quite yet in the EU. There were also a lot of cars going through from Croatia. We were a little miffed at having been closely searched, but we were not used to border controls within the EU, so it was a new experience.

We had a lovely drive through Austria, Bavaria and into France with two pleasant overnight stops, one of them in one of our favourite places, Oberammergau in Bavaria. Apart from the setting in the lovely mountains, there are the wonderful woodcarving shops and the delightful murals and trompe l'oeil paintings on their houses. Oberammergau is famous for their "Passion Plays", which are performed by the villagers every ten years, but it is also a ski resort and a tourist haven in the summer. Nearby is some stunning scenery and plenty of places to visit, including the famous castle of "Neuschwannstein". We always stayed in the same hotel, the dog friendly Hotel Wolf, where on the dinner tables, they put little pots of pork dripping with bits of crackling mixed in, which when spread on fresh bread is an excellent appetiser before the meal, though probably not good for you.

Arriving in France, our house-hunting base was a little cottage lent to us in the village of Gluges on the Dordogne and it wasn't long before we were looking at numerous houses with a variety of estate agents around the region. We saw some really lovely properties but they were mainly too isolated for us; we wanted to be near some "life". One of the estate agents was Louise, an English girl, who had built up her business in Beaulieu sur Dordogne and who had shown us a house on the river the previous year. This we had bid for but had lost it to a French woman. Even Louise was unable to show us anything we particularly liked, but then one day the house on the river was up for sale again. The story was that the couple who had bought it and were living together in what was their first love nest, were splitting up.

At first we were not interested, as we had put our previous disappointment behind us a long time ago and we had already found a house by the water in Croatia, so that was no longer a criteria. After seeing more houses we did not like, and getting more frustrated, we asked Louise to put in a bid for the house on the river; having looked at it again from the other side of the river it kindled all our previous liking for the house.

Alas, it was not to be. When Louise telephoned she was told that the house had been sold through the internet to an English couple.

The month of April sped by and so did the images of numerous houses before our tired eyes. However, we had an appointment to stay at my daughter Nicky's in England in early May to look after grandchildren so it was a welcome relief to have a break from house hunting. After a week we had phone call from Louise.
'You are not going to believe this!' she started.
'Try me', I said.
'The house on the river is back on the market'. I was dumbfounded.
'I had better speak to March and phone you back'.

At first March was not interested, having been through two disappointments, but after a lot of discussion, we eventually resolved to put in our bid which was accepted. A meeting with the Notaire in France, to sign the papers and pay the deposit, was arranged for the end of May and this, duly completed, meant the house was ours(in France it is very costly for the seller to back out at this stage). The final paperwork and payment was to be completed at the end of August so we had three months to kill. What better than to spend the summer in our house by the sea, so we packed up the car again and headed back to Croatia.

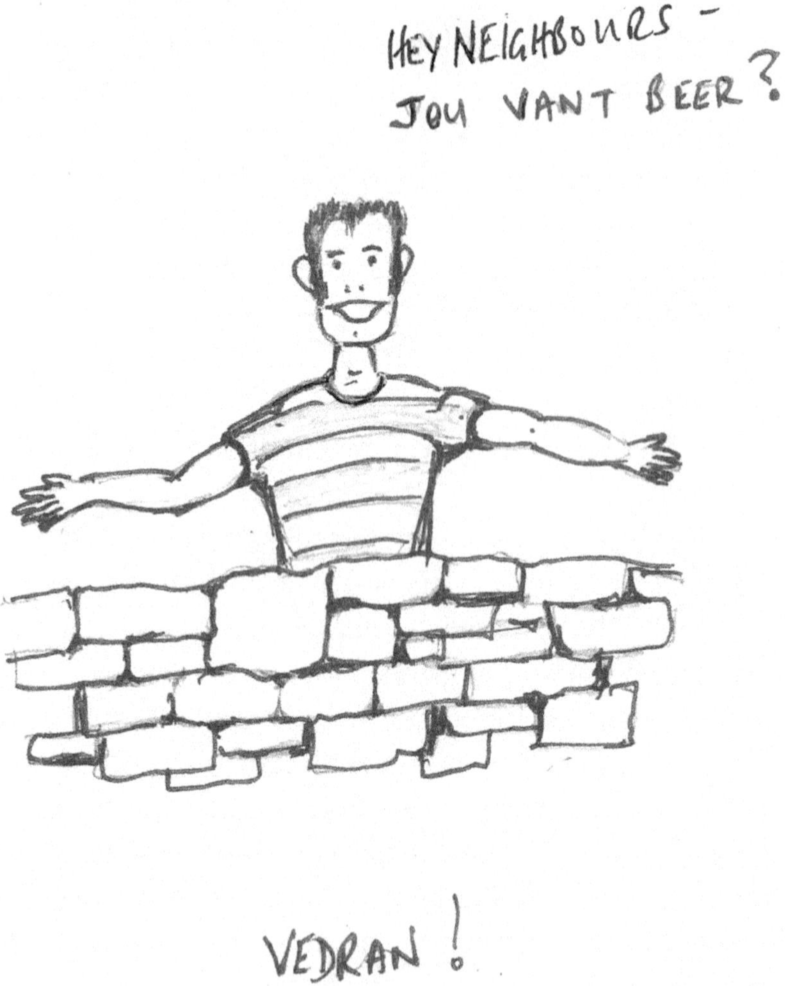
HEY NEIGHBOURS -
JOU VANT BEER?
VEDRAN!

Chapter 8

Kate and Vedran

We were able to set off back to Croatia in the first few days of June and had decided to try a completely new route. We had heard that there was a regular ferry service from Ancona in Italy, across the Adriatic to Split. There were two main ferry companies on the route with one or the other providing an overnight crossing every night. I reckoned that Ancona was about a fifteen-hour drive from the Dordogne so an overnight stop was in order; gone were the days when I would not have flinched at such a drive!

The Mont Blanc tunnel was closed after the bad fire there, so we headed for the Frejus tunnel further to the west and stayed overnight in Modane, just on the French side of the tunnel. Modane was a soulless looking town. It had a big railway terminus and had been on the major road route through to Italy but had now been bypassed. A town with just the one road along the valley, it had seen better days, but to our relief we found quite a good Logis hotel with a restaurant opposite the railway station.

We were travelling again with a fully laden car of clothing, our art materials and things for the house, with some of it in the box on the roof. When there is no hotel garage we always worry that the car will be broken into and everything taken. We took in as much as we could but I had a bad night's sleep, waking up regularly and getting out of bed to look down from our window to the car in the street below.

The next morning we were through the tunnel early and into Italy, winding our way down the steep valley, which leads to Turin. Around Turin we encountered five tolls on the motorway. At one of these I missed the lane for credit cards and ended up in a cash only lane, spending the next few minutes rummaging in various pockets purses and bags to find enough for the toll. Eventually they accepted a mixture of British, French and Italian money. This was going to be so much easier when the euro started in a few months.

The Italian motorways were busier than the British ones with a frightening number of lorries often on routes with only two lanes. The stretch from Modena to Bologna through to Cesena was particularly terrifying. In comparison the French motorways were a dream. After Rimini, thankfully things got much better, with less traffic and drivers going at more sensible speeds. It was a lovely hot sunny day and the drive down the coast past San Marino was picturesque and more relaxing.

The big, busy port at Ancona was easy to find and having parked at the terminal I went to book our passage for that night. I found the Jadrolinija desk in a smart booking hall and using our faithful visa paid about £100 for the car, two people and a cabin. This amazed me as we had been used to paying double that for a one-hour trip on the expensive bit of water between Jersey and St Malo in France. Jadrolinija I noted was also the company who seemed to have the monopoly on all the ferry crossings to all the islands on the Dalmatian coast.

It was only five pm so we had made good time in spite of the traffic. We were able to board the boat at seven pm but also had first to get our passports and boarding cards checked by the Italian police, also at seven pm. We had time to walk Rupert around the harbour and also to have a beer. Ancona was a big commercial port and had a modern ferry terminal with cafes and restaurants but it was obviously not big enough for the trade. The car park was full so cars were parked everywhere causing all sorts of problems.

The ferries were coming and going on every birth , mostly it seemed, to Greece. There also seemed to be little control on the embarkation procedure. Cars and lorries were constantly vying for position and hooting and jostling to get on the boats first with little control from the police or harbour officials. From our position in a bar on the quay we could see this entire drama taking place so resolved to position ourselves and car as close to the ferry as we could. The ferry, the Marco Polo, was already moored next to the terminal so we knew what we had to do. I made my way to the police desk early so was near to the front of the queue when they opened but this did not mean that it was going to be a speedy process.

The people in front of me were Bosnians who were

given a thorough grilling. They had to produce additional documents and the policeman at the desk seemed to spend an age on the computer. Eventually I got to the desk with our passports and boarding cards. The policeman looked at the passports briefly, stamped our boarding cards and smiled wishing me a good trip. Such is the power of a European Community passport I thought.

There was no queue for the boat, just a mass of cars in a broad phalanx close to the rear doors of the ferry. When the first car was signalled to move forward, everyone moved. The police, customs officials and ferry crew all shouted and waved their arms to try to get some order and eventually we progressed onto the boat. Why every one was so agitated and anxious to get on so quickly, when they had tickets and we had two hours before the boat sailed totally defeated us. This was definitely the Latin mentality in action! We then had the shouting and waving to get our car into the right position on the car deck but eventually we had moved into our little cabin, and after a quick wash, we were enjoying a well-earned drink in the very comfortable bar. We were amazed that for little a over a pound I had a large glass of red wine and March had a cherry brandy; this was going to be a good night!

The restaurant opened at eight pm so we adjourned to see what they had to offer. We managed to get a table next to a window overlooking the harbour and decided to go for the set menu, as we were quite hungry after a long day. We started with a small portion of spaghetti Bolognese followed by a wiener schnitzel, accompanied by chips and mixed salad. For the dessert we chose a fruit tart and cream. We washed all this down with an excellent bottle of red wine from Peljesac, which is an island to the south of Brac, not far from Dubrovnik. The food was plain but good, the waiters were in black tie, very friendly, and the restaurant was pleasant and clean. We were pleasantly surprised and more than happy when we climbed into our bunks.

We were up and about by the break of dawn. We, and Rupert, were enjoying a stroll around the deck and delighted in the superb scenery of sea and numerous islands as the boat neared Split. Many of the islands, Croatia has over a thousand, were uninhabited but many had little fishing ports and coastal communities. Some of the smaller ones had just one large property, probably a monastery, or a lighthouse complex. Sailing through these islands as dawn was breaking was one of our most memorable experiences. It was seven thirty before we drove off the boat at Split harbour.

Things were a bit better organised than in Ancona and we soon in a proper queue to go through customs. First we had our passports checked by a policeman and then again by a friendly customs man who asked the usual questions of whether we had anything to declare. He was happy with Rupert's documents and was waving us away when an older official came out of the building and said our car was heavily laden and we must pay duty on the things we had brought to Croatia. We insisted that everything was either clothing or well used items for our house on Brac.

'You must buy in Croatia', he demanded.

'I agree', I reposted, 'we have bought everything for our house in Croatia, these are just items we had spare and we could not find in Croatia'.

'You must pay', he insisted.

'I'm not paying', I said (I had been told that you must be tough with Croatian officials). There then followed an animated discussion between the old and young customs officials; we could tell from the body language that the younger one was all for letting us go and fortunately he won the argument.

It wasn't long before we were across on the ferry to the island and driving on to Povlja. As we drove down the steep winding road to the village we again saw that wonderful view of the village and harbour, the clear blue sea and the mountains of the mainland. We never ceased to love this view. Driving along the harbour several of the villagers waved to us, including the Dutch couple, whom we noticed had their smart restaurant up and running. As we drove into our drive, the gates were open; Robi and Erica were there waiting and waving. They were really pleased to see us and we them.

'We knew you had arrived', said Erica, 'Somebody phone us!'

Erica had opened the doors and windows to air the house and our bed was made up. Our house looked lovely in the warm sunshine.

'Lemons ready for picking', said Robi pointing to the lemon tree mural I had painted in our porch.

'You come have drink before you offload.'

We were soon catching up on the village gossip over a glass of wine. We sat in the outside area to their restaurant, which was now open and looked very inviting with their stone tables under their wooden pagodas, which were covered in various flowering plants.

The most interesting gossip for us was that the Dutch, who had had the entire village behind them when we left, were now really disliked by most of the villagers. They had failed to honour the level of wages promised to their staff and some of the local small builders still had not been paid for work. This was particularly crippling for one young chap who was not able to buy any more materials until he paid the supplier. They had also encroached onto neighbours land with dustbins and washing hanging out.

One other sore point was that the local council had agreed to the closing of the harbour opposite their restaurant to traffic after seven pm. This was quite a nuisance for most of the villagers who lived on the other side and who had to make a big detour to get out of the village. There was more, but in general they were now not well liked, so much so that they had been given nicknames; he was called the "thief" and she the "devil".

We had to get to grips with unpacking, but before departing we booked a table for lunch. We were not only looking forward to one of Erica's pizzas but had no intention of cooking lunch ourselves.

We were back at the restaurant by one o'clock. Erica appeared with a lovely looking girl with long black hair and a delightful happy face.

'This is Kate', she announced. 'She is our waitress for the summer'.

Kate chatted to us as we looked through the menu. She was bubbly and cheerful and told us that she was studying English at university in Split. Her English was already good but she asked if she could come to talk to us every evening before she had to start at the restaurant. We thought her English was very good but she said that the standard was so high that she may struggle to pass her exams. We were very happy to oblige.

The atmosphere in the restaurant was happy and cheerful. Robi was naturally a happy fellow but Kate and Erica were always laughing about something and always had a cheerful word for every table.

We then noticed a young man serving at one of the tables and asked Erica who he was. 'That is Mario from the village. He is a university student. He vork for us during the holidays'.

Mario came over to say hello and chatted to us in excellent English. He was a pleasant young man with a cheerful personality and was a very good waiter. We could see that we were going to be regular customers that summer; it would also relieve me of some cooking even though I enjoyed it.

Robi also had another business. Using his garage as a workshop he made leather or plastic folders for menus, diaries, wallets and folders for many different uses. Quite a lot of his business was for the restaurant and hotel trade and his orders were growing steadily. He now had to employ one or two people to manufacture and assemble the products so that he could be free to run the restaurant. One of his employees that summer was Vedran.

We met Vedran the next day when he leaned over the wall and introduced himself. He was about thirty, good looking, simple in outlook and a born comedian. Lucie, the girl who had found the house for us, referred to him in a derogatory way as "sex on legs"; he certainly fancied his chances with the girls. He was also burdened with a stammer, but that did not stem his endless chatter and jokes. I suppose one could call him a likeable rogue. Vedran took to calling to us over the partition stone wall whenever he saw us in our garden or on the terrace: 'Hey neighbours, wwwould you like bbbbeer'.

After the first acceptance to be friendly, we later declined his offers of beers or ice creams, as we found that he was raiding them from Robi's restaurant fridge! However we would occasionally go up to the restaurant during his breaks and buy a beer for us all and listen to his stories and jokes.

The day after we arrived Kate came down to our house at about five pm to have her English "lessons", but not proper lessons as such, more discussions about a variety of topics. The first day she wanted to talk about Henry VIII and his wives. This really stretched our memories, as it was many years since we had covered that part of history at school, though fortunately we had read a book a few years before on the subject. Mostly though we chatted about what life was like in England. Like most young Croatians we met this was what they most wanted to know.

Occasionally we would still be on the beach as it was so hot, even at five o'clock that the best place was in the water. But this did not deter Kate; as she would come down to join us in the sea and on the beach just to talk in English.

One day she appeared and was quite flustered. She had seen a naked woman on the beach not far from where we were bathing. Kate had apparently told the woman that she should not be on the beach naked, as this was not allowed on a family beach. The woman, a German, told Kate that it was a natural thing to be naked and then to Kate's utter embarrassment handed her a camera and asked Kate to take a photograph of her. Apparently she wanted to compare how her figure looked from last year. Kate quickly took the picture, handed back the camera, and walked away as quickly as she could. We agreed with Kate.

We were both against nudity on family beaches, including topless women. We could not see why we should have suffer ugly, naked bodies (as they mostly were) thrust upon our vision and ruining the landscape.

It is strange how things come in twos or threes. The next morning, for a change, we decided to swim further along the beach, on the other side of the Punta. There were never more than a handful of people there, though our own beach in front of the house was never what you could call crowded; I doubt if I ever saw more than twenty people at any one time. We had become quite keen snorkellers since we had arrived and bought a set of gear each from our local shop.

As we swam and dived between the rocks, March just ahead of me signalled excitedly to her front. I swam up to her and then saw in the clear water about twenty feet away, a fat naked woman standing in the water up to her armpits and just beyond her a man with a similar naked fat flabby figure. As stealthily as we could we swam back the way we came barely able to keep our mirth under control, particularly as we were sure it was some people who had house not far from us. Not a pretty sight, but at least they had found a secluded spot to indulge in their naturism.

The weather was glorious and the sea, already over twenty degrees, seemed to be getting warmer every day. We did a great deal of snorkelling amongst the rocks in front of our house and marvelled at the thousands of small fish, which swam all around us. Often there would be enormous shoals of them almost stationary around us and one could just swim through them as they moved aside to let one through. There were fish of many sizes, shapes and colours. I had been a trained compressed air diver in my early days in the army and had dived in many lakes, rivers and seas but I reckoned that the Adriatic sea around Brac was the clearest and cleanest I had experienced. March was enthralled with all the fish and her first experience of snorkelling.

As she floated on the surface with arms and legs akimbo, watching the fish beneath her, she said to herself: 'Heaven is not so far away'.

It wasn't long before we adopted a summer routine.

As the sun streamed through the chinks of our bedroom shutters early in the morning, we were soon up and about. After breakfast on the terrace, we usually set about our housekeeping duties, which mainly consisted of sweeping and then mopping the tiled floors throughout the house. This accomplished, we would set off on foot to the village to get any bread and groceries we needed. This had to be done earlier in the morning rather than later as it became too hot for us to walk in the sun even for a ten-minute stroll there and back.

Rupert was also keen to keep out of the heat of the day, spending most of the afternoons in the house, which remained quite cool if we remembered to close the shutters on the sunny side of the house. After shopping we would usually have a coffee at one of the quayside café/bars and watch the tourists strolling about. Many of them were off the small tourist boats, which came across from Brela or Baska Voda on the mainland, just opposite Povlja. Some boats stayed for an hour or so that the tourists could stroll around, visit the church and visit a café.

One of the boats stayed much longer and moored opposite the Dok bar. There, by arrangement with Mr Dok, the captain would cook lunch on Mr Dok's BBQ whilst the passengers had a drink in the bar. The visitors seemed to be from many different parts of Europe, including Germans, Czechs, Poles and on one occasion we met a young English couple on honeymoon. They were absolutely amazed to meet us as we were the first people from the UK they had met so far. The reluctance of the Brits to go to Croatia, which many still regarded as a war zone, was still there, and it was going to take a lot of advertising and publicity to change this attitude.

We were usually home by ten with plenty of time left of the morning to indulge in our various artistic pursuits; March at her sewing machine concocting a machine-embroidery and me at my easel in the shaded side of the house.

Before lunch, which was anytime between one and two pm, we always had a swim in the sea just opposite the house. After a shower, we would then lunch on the terrace under our tent/gazebo thing, which we had brought from England. If we were lucky we would have freshly caught fish, grilled on our large stone BBQ, which looked more like a German bunker than a grill but then they all have them in Dalmatia. Most have a chimney on the top and are big enough to roast a small sheep on a spit. Whether we had fish was pretty hit and miss.

If the "Povlja", the village's only commercial boat had come in as usual at about ten am and had some fish to spare, we would be waiting on the quay to buy anything they had. More often than not it was sardines but we more than happy with that. A kilo of sardines was about ten kunas or eighty pence.

In the absence of fish we usually had a salad. We were now able to get lettuce and their large beefsteak tomatoes were as tasty as I remembered from the days when tomatoes tasted like tomatoes and not like the tasteless supermarket rubbish we get nowadays. After lunch we indulged in the wonderful continental tradition of the siesta. Usually we took this on our loungers either under a parasol or our olive tree. The rest of the afternoon we spent in the see communing with the fish.

Occasionally we would have to do something strenuous such as going off to Selca or Bol to the markets there or to get some more money from the bank or the cash-point or top up the car with petrol; this was a rare occasion as a full tank usually lasted well over a month.

Our evenings were spent having a quiet meal and a drink on our terrace or occasionally wandering to the village or to Robi and Erica's restaurant for a drink, if they were not too busy. June passed in this rather lazy but very pleasant life style though I managed to complete several paintings of the scenery and some stunning sunsets. March also was productive in her fabric art.

RAAADEEEEO BRAAACH!

Chapter 9

Radeeeo Braaaach

Moving into July we noticed the increase in the number of tourists around the village and also at Robi and Erica's restaurant, though one could hardly call it busy. It was quite a short season where the majority of tourists came in the three months from June to August, so that was when the tourist industry had to make its money.

Some of the bigger resorts on the mainland had a slightly longer season but it was not significant. The continentals tend to take their holidays mostly in these three months with August being the most popular, particularly for the Italians, who were yet to arrive.

The number of tourist boats bringing tourists from the mainland increased. We would see them passing our house on the way into the harbour from the mainland. Some of the bigger ones looked very much like old-fashioned pirate galleons with two or three masts, rigging and usually folded sails. Their wooden superstructures were quite magnificent and very well crafted. The wood was highly varnished and well cared for. Some did just day trips but the much larger ones were for cruising and were equipped with small cabins. The little harbours up and down the Dalmatian coast were full of these splendid looking craft so the business was obviously good.

We also saw many more yachts arriving either just for an hour or so, or mooring overnight. Povlja was an ideal haven for an overnight stop and indeed so were most of the many little harbours dotted around Brac and the many other islands. One problem though was the limited moorings in what was quite a big natural harbour. There were water and electricity terminals along the harbour but most of the space was taken by the numerous small fishing boats owned by the villagers. A visiting yacht would have difficulty in finding a space.

We were having a Plinkovac or two one evening in the Dutch restaurant and we watched a yacht having difficulty mooring nearby. We noticed the red ensign so knew they were Brits and when they came across to the bar and took the next table we introduced ourselves. They seemed pleased to be able to chat to their country-folk and said what a wonderful sailing holiday they were having on their chartered boat, but they did say that they almost sailed on to the next port when they were having difficulties mooring.

By chance Susy and her Army boyfriend Simon, a sailing instructor with the British Army based in Povlja, came to sit near to us. We related the experience of the English couple and asked why there was a problem over moorings. It turned out that everyone who lived along the harbour insisted that the space opposite their houses was their space to moor their boats.

Many of the people in the village appreciated the need to attract visiting yachts but nobody, nor the local commune officials, was prepared to take any action to organise the moorings so that there were plenty of moorings for visitors.

'Nothing ever get done here', said Susy, 'Everyone argue too much'. Simon said that he would love to get his hands on the reorganisation of the moorings as Povlja was such a super place for visiting yachts, but they would also need some showers and lavatories.

*

We were still enjoying Croatian TV with all their British and American films and comedy programmes but I had difficulty in finding a radio station, which did not have endless chatter in Croatian between the music. I had failed to get the BFBS channel, the British forces radio which they received at the hotel, probably due to the hill between the harbour and the Punta, and the limited range of their transmission.

Then one day I came across a station, which played almost non-stop good music. Eventually we heard a greasy male American voice saying, 'Radeeeo Braaaach', and occasionally 'We're playing more music' (though what this meant we were not sure, more than whom?) or 'You too can have an <u>American</u> radio station in your city' or 'This programme has come to you from the voice of America'.

All a little nauseating and rather condescending and patronising in tone, but they did at least play good music most of the time. However, that summer, Tom Jones was having a great success with his new hit record "Sex Bomb", which was being played on every station, but on Radio Brac about a dozen times a day. Much as we had liked Tom Jones in the past, we were pretty fed up with this record and it was a race to get to the radio to turn it off when Tom started up. But we were not let off that easily. At Erica and Robi's they were usually playing Radio Dalmatia who also played "Sex Bomb" ad nauseu, but in the kitchen Erica and Kate, who laughed and sang to the music all day, accompanied all the hit songs including Tom's.

Croatian TV had also borrowed some ideas from BBC and ITV. One of these was "Ready Steady Cook". The set was almost identical and the routine the same, however, what differed drastically was the type of food and the imagination and standard of the chefs. The results were really quite terrible with little or no ideas on artistic presentation (sometimes you can disguise an indifferent meal with a little artistic flair) and in some cases the food looked pretty inedible.

Even as an enthusiastic amateur cook, I had to laugh. These programmes made us realise what a lot of talented chefs we had in the UK and how far we had progressed in haut quisine since the last war. Food in restaurants at home and in Jersey had improved dramatically and in many ways we were now bettering the French whose restaurants in many places had lost their previous high standards.

Nevertheless, the Croatian chefs on that particular programme had a lot to learn about cooking from the western Europeans, though we could have named one or two Croatian chefs from various restaurants who were better qualified to be on "Ready Steady Cook" than the bunch they were using. In general they excel at grilled fish and meat with salads, and whole lambs or goats on a spit, but they are not into interesting sauces.

There had also been an influx of American TV series on their TV. "Frasier" was a welcome addition, but many of those with actors from the present generation such as "Buffy the Vampire Slayer" all seemed to demonstrate that the younger generation in America had changed their accents; much like a similar revolution in the UK. The girls and young women in particular all spoke with squeaky "Donald Duck" voices, and very quickly. These were not the accents of the Hollywood stars of previous years. At first I thought that the Croatian TV were playing the tapes at the wrong, and faster speed. A lot of the time we had great difficulty in understanding what was being said. March and I would walk about the house trying very hard to imitate these funny voices but failing miserably and ending up in fits of giggles, but we still said 'Hi' to one another in squeaky "Donald Duck" voices.

Whilst on the subject of TV we were sitting on our terrace one day when two young men came through our gate and approached us. They spoke in Croatian, but we asked if they spoke English, to which they replied that they had a 'leetle' English and that they were something to do with TV. Beyond that we were not sure what they were wanting. We quickly called Robi who came down to our house and spoke to the two men.

'They vant TV licence money you know', he said.

'How much', we replied.

'Four hundred kunas (then about £31) but I say you only here a short time each year'.

Robi continued to talk animatedly to them. Arguing with Robi must have been like arguing with a brass band (to quote from a description of Churchill by one of his adversaries). His arms waved and his voice grew louder.

Suddenly he stopped and said triumphantly: 'You pay two hundred kunas only'.

This we did in cash and received an official receipt, which Robi checked. But that was not the end of it. They then asked for Robi's licence money, which prompted Robi into another of his harangues with the two young men looking quite abashed.

In the end he paid only the same as we did, although they wanted more from him as a permanent resident. His argument, he later told us was that he had said they were so busy that they never watched TV. Bartering in this way for such things as TV licences seemed so alien but really quite amusing. We got the impression that if we hadn't been there we would have escaped payment for a year.

News was apparently spreading quickly around the village on their excellent intelligence network that the Licence men were about. People were closing shutters and locking doors, pretending they were away, including Lijeka our other close neighbour, who was shuttered up and nowhere to be seen! Whether they ever caught up with everyone we could only speculate, but it seemed a tremendous game.

*

We saw quite a lot of interesting things from our terrace. One day we noticed a fire on the lower slopes of the mountains on the mainland opposite our house. We could see that it was getting worse and seemed to be getting closer to a small community on the hillside. Then we heard the aeroplanes, which were two twin-engined turboprops painted in a bright yellow similar to the "yellow perils" which fly between Jersey and Guernsey but these were a seaplane variety. They swooped down to the sea and flew along touching the surface collecting water and then up to the side of the hill, depositing their watery load over the fire.

They were pretty accurate in their targeting but still had to keep up the operation for over an hour. It was good entertainment for the tourists on the beach and those enjoying their food in the restaurant. It even brought out Vedran from his work in Robi's garage and prompted his usual call to us: 'Hey neighbours, you want a beer maybe'. But we declined having already charged our glasses during the entertainment.

It was only a couple of days after the fire incident that we had further entertainment across the sea towards the mainland. Erica had come down to the house saying that she had seen on the TV that there were two whales off the coast near Makarska and that they were moving along the coast to our front. It was thought that the whales were lost amongst the islands and plans were being made to try to guide them to the open Adriatic. It was hoped that they would follow a passing ship, as they sometimes do, to the open sea and this was being organised.

In the meantime we watched, through our binoculars, the two whales swimming about surrounded by a large flotilla of small boats until eventually they disappeared out of sight. We later learned that the ship-following operation had been a success. The incident prompted me to ask Erica if any big sharks had ever been sighted near the island.

'Ve don't have sharks here,' she said to my relief.

'One was seen by Split about fifteen years ago and all German tourists went home,' and she continued: 'Locals said, if ve had known it vas dat easy to get rid of Germans, ve vould have said the sea was full of sharks during the var!'

We noticed that many of the tourists were Czechs who had all driven down through Austria and Zagreb. A few families were staying in various apartments at the Punta including with Lijeka next door. One family arrived whilst we relaxing on our terrace and offloaded their car, which was full of food of every description including bread, all of which they had brought with them. Lijeka told us that they had iceboxes full of frozen food and had asked her if it could go in her freezer. The locals were not very happy with the Czechs, not only because they brought most of their food with them, but they spent very little in the shops, cafes and restaurants.

We later heard that Croatian customs were getting very tough with them at the borders by either confiscating food or making them pay a customs duty. The Czech travel agencies had also driven very hard bargains for accommodation but the locals were so desperate for tourists that they had accepted the low prices. In the absence of western Europeans in any significant numbers, except for the Italians who only came in August anyway, the Czechs and some Poles were the only ones around.

The tourist industry desperately needed western Europeans and Americans with their spending power to give it a boost. We were pleased to see in some of the British newspapers we got from the army that some articles were beginning to appear about Croatia and these were very favourable. In one article it said that Croatia was one of the last tourist locations where a woman could travel quite safely on her own without fear of being molested. This was certainly true.

Early one morning in July, March woke me to say that there was a strange noise outside. After gathering my senses I heard what sounded like bubbling noise, which I first thought was rain but the more I listened to it the more confused I became. Putting on our dressing gowns we ventured outside onto the terrace in the gathering light of dawn and looked around and listened. Looking out to sea we then saw, about half a mile out, a great turbulence in the sea making the bubbling, thrashing noise. At first we thought the worst. Could this be something to with an earthquake or perhaps an underwater volcano!

We then realised as we threw off our sleepiness and our brains began to respond that it had to be an enormous shoal of small fish. A few fishing boats hovered around the phenomenon and more were arriving from the village as the bubbling swirled around, occasionally totally subsiding and then reappearing somewhere else.

There must have been thousands of small fish to have caused such a disturbance in the sea. It was then that Robi and Erica appeared sleepy-eyed on their terrace behind and above us.

'Vat is dis,' said Robi peering out to sea.

'Ah, fishes – tuna chase dem!' he exclaimed.

They had probably seen this all before but to us it was an amazing sight. The fishermen were of course having a field day and no doubt their families would be eating sardines all week. The phenomenon stayed around for almost all the morning, dying down for a while and then reappearing further along the coast at intervals.

Spectating from our terrace continued to give us a great deal of interest. Many of the locals came for a stroll out to the Punta and we also had the occasional visit from the girl at the post office, who finished for the day at 3pm and brought out any mail to the residents at the Punta. Everyone was friendly and always smiled to us up on our terrace and said "dobar dan" (good day) often pointing to the sun and saying "dobro", that well used word meaning anything which is good.

One spectacle, which we had observed every day

was a woman driving an old Jugo, which turned at great speed on Robi's small restaurant car park, spitting out pebbles from the tyres. We noticed that she was the employee at the hotel who had said to us in early January when we asked for a room: 'No tourists!' She had an unpronounceable Croatian name but it sounded a bit like Georgina so that is what we called her.

We had eventually got to know her when we occasionally went for a beer in the hotel bar, but why did she drive out of the village every day and turn round in the car park, disappearing back to the village. After one occasion we asked Erica over the garden wall if she knew what Georgina was doing.

'She just passed driving test but she no good at reversing so she turn around here!' said Erica laughing.

There was another very old small fiat, which did the same thing with an old man driving, but his problem we discovered was that his reverse gear was not working.

On Saturdays the army captain and his instructors, about a dozen of them, became regular visitors for a meal at Robi and Erica's. We had become quite friendly with the captain, Danny, who always invited us to these sessions and he was a regular visitor to our house. I was so pleased that the soldiers were always so well behaved and their presence around the village, or on the water, was not obtrusive. There were those in the village though who did not want the army there but they were forgetting the thirty or so local people who had work in the hotel, plus the income generated in the village shops, restaurants and bars in the evenings.

Danny also kept me informed of everything that was going on in the army so it was good to keep in touch, particularly as I had enjoyed my career in the army.

Robi was also serving steaks and any fish that were available, plus he now had chips. Whilst Erica handled the pizzas from the kitchen, Robi cooked the steaks and the fish in his large grill and bar outside. We had found the beef steaks we had bought from the butcher a little tough but Robi's were very tender, so one Saturday I asked him what was his secret.

'I put steaks in dish of corn oil, you know, not olive oil, you know, for one week in fridge.' (Robi used "you know" quite a lot)

We certainly tried this and had the same tasty and tender result. This secret should be passed on to some of the French establishments serving up "steak-frites" where the steaks are as tough as old boots.

*

Towards the end of July Povlja held its first festival since the Balkan war had ended. There were various processions and events during the day but the main event was a big party on the quay at the end of the harbour. There was a big stage on which three bands played in succession and stalls were set up selling cooked food and others selling drinks. Robi had set up a bar with tables, chairs and large parasols the brewery had lent him. We of course went down to see the fun at about 8pm. All the bars and restaurants were full and people were beginning to gather for the musical entertainment.

We bought beers from Vedran who was Robi's barman for the evening and settled down to do some people watching and enjoy the beer. It was a warm evening and as the night closed in the harbour lights and the lights from the village and cafes reflected on the still water in the harbour; it was a lovely sight.

At about 11pm Robi received a call on his mobile from Erica, who was still holding the fort at their restaurant, that March's daughter Marika had called from Jersey saying that the vet in France had said there was something wrong with Rupert. He had a blood test before we left there so that his rabies inoculation could be verified as successful. We immediately went into panic and raced back to Erica to hear the message first hand and then phoned Marika, who said that Richard, March's son in Luxembourg, had heard from Louise our estate agent in France, who in turn had had a message from the vet that Rupert had rabies.

We were initially distraught but the more we talked it over with Erica at the restaurant the more we began to doubt the accuracy of the message. Rupert was fine and very lively and healthy as usual and showing no signs of rabies symptoms, however, we could not check until the following day as we only had the vet's surgery number. I was convinced that, because so many people had handled the message, it had become transformed rather like the old army example of "send reinforcements we are going to advance, ending up at the destination after being relayed several times, as send three and fourpence we are going to a dance."

Nevertheless, we had a worrying night with March not

sleeping very much and cuddling Rupert close to her on the bed. Our fears fortunately were unfounded. The phial containing Rupert's blood sample was contaminated so the tests could not be carried out at the laboratory. We had to go back to the vet when we got back to France and Rupert would have to have another rabies jab and blood test.

*

July melted away in the lovely sunshine to herald August with even hotter weather, and the Italians. They came over in their droves no doubt leaving Italy with only old people and dogs to look after the shop. They were happier, noisier, better spenders and better dressed than eastern Europeans and they certainly filled Robi and Erica's restaurant at both lunchtime and evenings, where they demanded fish. They were no doubt up to their eyeballs in pizzas in Italy, so fish was what they craved.

In spite of the numbers, the music and the endless chatter, we were pleasantly surprised that very little of the noise drifted down to our house. We were usually in bed by eleven pm, being early risers, and could not hear anything from the restaurant even though it was still full; my earlier fears when we bought the house, that the noise could be a problem, were unfounded. For a change we enjoyed the buzz of having people about. Sitting on our terrace on those balmy warm evenings, sipping a glass of wine and watching the tourists going up the little road past our house to the restaurant and trying to guess their nationalities, became our regular evening pastime.

With the temperatures in the higher thirties, we were spending much more time in the sea communing with the fish. The nights were also hot and sticky. We had bought the only fan for sale in the little hardware shop in Selca, and as we had also searched in Bol and Supetar, we were sure it was the only one on the Island. But this was hardly enough to keep us cool. I had made mosquito screens with wooden frames and fine netting we had brought from France. These fitted into the spaces in the window frames between windows and shutters so that we could have windows and shutters wide open to take advantage of any sea breeze which might be around.

We were pleasantly surprised how few mosquitoes we saw but we did have some small flies, which occasionally bit in the evenings, particularly on bare legs. However if we remembered to rub on our suntan cream, which contained an anti insect repellent, there was no problem.

Erica frequently joined us as we chatted with Kate in the evenings, before the restaurant opened and we had some amusing discussions on all sorts of subjects.

One evening as the two girls arrived, I asked them: 'Would you like an aperitif?'

Erica burst into a fit of giggles and said ' I don't understand, what teeth?' with a puzzled expression.

'Aperitif !' I said slowly

'A drink!'

Erica continued to laugh, but spluttered out: 'I thought you said, vould we like pair of teeth!'

August drew to a close in glorious sunshine. The sea was now 27 degrees centigrade and swimming occupied most of our time from morning until night. But alas we had to get back to France to sign the final contract for the house at the Notaire's so with great reluctance we said goodbye to all our friends and our house.

Chapter 10

Weather Reports from Erika

We drove through the village, along the harbour and waved goodbye to people we had met. Suzy's father and mother were walking along the harbour with Franika, the grandmother who did our cleaning and gardening. We stopped to say our farewells. None of them spoke much English but we got by with the occasional "dobro" and we were surprised to see that they were genuinely sorry to see us go, wanting to know when we would return. We promised to return as soon as we could and drove on to the end of the harbour where a group of locals were playing the usual cards and sipping their beer. Tonko saw us and leaped up to say good-bye. With him we only spoke German, which he spoke fluently. He insisted that we drove up to his house with him following, as there was something he wanted to give us.

We arrived at his house, which had a glorious view of the harbour, the sea and the mountains from up above the village and pressed upon us glasses of slivovic, which he had made. We knew that protesting was of no use so we accepted gracefully. He then showed us his wine cellar, which was stocked with his own wine, olive oil and various strong unpronounceable concoctions. He took various bottles from the shelves to give to us, including a bottle of olive oil, which we knew we would prize as their olive oil from their local olive groves was quite the best we had ever tasted. Fortunately we had plenty of time so a few minutes sipping our drinks and chatting to Tonko and his wife Dalmina on their terrace was a pleasant farewell to Povlja.

We dragged ourselves away and set off on the drive to Supetar to catch the ferry to the mainland. As usual we saw only a handful of cars on the road; most of them again in the middle of the road but reached Supetar unscathed at eleven o'clock, in time to pay our electricity bill. But alas when we arrived at the gate, which was manned by an attendant (what they were protecting we were not quite sure) who said in broken English: 'Everybody go breakfast, come back in hour.'

We had become used to this sort of thing so in did not annoy us anymore. Still chuckling we settled down in a café on the quay to pass the time. In due course we paid the electricity bill and returned to the harbour for a leisurely fish lunch with still plenty of time to catch the 3 o'clock ferry. We had taken the precaution of putting our car in the ferry queue early as this ferry was usually busy and oversubscribed with many cars left on the quay, though in the summer they just kept running the ferries to take up the backlog.

In Split we relaxed in a little café close to the terminal to read our books to wait for the overnight ferry to Ancona to start embarking at seven pm. Sitting there I suddenly noticed a couple sitting at a table across from us. They were very gypsy in looks though very well dressed. Then the man grinned and showed full rows of teeth top and bottom all in gold. It was a fascinating sight and March too was intrigued. We watched him for some time as surreptitiously as we could without raising suspicion that we were over interested in his teeth as a future investment (he no doubt had a defence plan to protect his teeth which no doubt included large knives). When they left, his wife who had had her back to us, also displayed a set of gold teeth but not all were gold so she was obviously only the back up in holding the family fortune. One had to speculate on how they redeemed their fortune in times if need. In hard times no doubt they were both toothless wonders.

The Croatian ferry, the Marco Polo, of the Jadrolinija Line was full that night, mostly with Italians who kept up an endless barrage of chatter everywhere. We went into dinner early and only just managed a table. We decided to spin the meal out as we had not been able to get a cabin mainly because we were travelling at the height of the tourist season. Taking the set meal, followed by coffee and grappa we eventually left the table just after midnight in search of some comfortable chair to read and doze as much as we could. We found some really good reclining seats in a little lounge with only a few people there but we soon realised why. The air conditioning was so powerful that after a while our feet were quite cold, so much so that we went for several strolls around the upper deck, which was packed with sleeping people in the hot night air; it was like walking into an oven.

Next morning we arrived in the port of Ancona in Italy. From the boat we could see the coast in the early morning sunlight and the port was bustling with activity. After breakfast we moved down to be near to the entrance to the car deck only to find an enormous queue stretching from a table, which had been positioned next to the door. Eventually the Italian police arrived and sat at the table to check documents and passports but when we eventually got to them they waved us on saying this was not a queue for European Community only for outsiders!! We squeezed into our car to await disembarkation but waited and waited without any signs of activity. The heat in the car deck was building up and the fumes were awful. Drivers were getting out of their cars and chattering but nothing happened in those awful conditions for over an hour. I was not surprised as we had seen the Italian police and Port authority people in action on our way out. Embarkation and disembarkation in Ancona was a disorganised mess. The "Crazy Gang" could have done better.

We drove through Italy on the autostrade, which was packed with lorries and businessmen racing to their next appointment. This was clearly quite "hairy" for me and not much fun; I enjoy driving mostly but this was enough to put us off from driving through Italy. However, once we had passed Bologna and Modena, the traffic eased and then after Turin we had a lovely climb up the valley to the Frejus tunnel. After a night stop in a little hotel in Montmelian near Chambery, we were in Beaulieu on the Dordogne in the early afternoon. We booked into one of the local hotels in time to relax and sort ourselves before our appointment the next day to sign the papers for the purchase of our "pied a terre" in France.

Things didn't go smoothly. When we got to the notaire he greeted us with:' Nous avon un problem'.

He had not received the final payment in his bank account so we could not complete the purchase. We quickly telephoned our bank in Jersey who confirmed that they had transferred the money and they had evidence that it had reached the main branch of the notaire's bank in Paris the day before so it was a problem on the French side. After the notaire had made a call to his local bank to confirm that the money was not there we rescheduled our meeting for three days later and went dejectedly back to the hotel. The owner of the hotel, who was also the lady we were buying the house from, was very sympathetic and insisted we had the keys to the house, saying that we could move in anyway as she was no doubt confident that everything would be sorted out in the next two days.

We hurriedly went out to buy two collapsible beds and decided to "camp" in the house. It was lovely and sunny, the river looked enchanting and we had electricity, water and bottled gas for cooking. The house was in "walk-in" condition though devoid of furniture so we were happy to move in.

Fortunately the next appointment with the notaire went smoothly and we signed the papers. He also admitted, and we also had evidence from our bank in Jersey, that his bank had the money on the day we had been in his office three days before!! (some friends of ours later said to us that it was common knowledge that French banks held onto international transfers for about 4 days to get more interest).

We had our house but no furniture. Coupled with our traumatic arrival in Croatia, our attempts to live on the continent seemed to be fraught with problems. The Jersey company who had stored our furniture and had agreed to ship it by the end of August now said that they could not deliver until 12th September. So we happily camped in our house by the river and enjoyed the sun. But that was not the end to our problems. The French lorry drivers decided to strike and as a result most of the petrol stations were closed, so the Jersey company got cold feet and said that they may not be able to come. Worse still, if they could not come the next scheduled delivery would be November.

I don't often get rattled, annoyed or blow my top. Most of the time I am pretty equable and have prided myself on my reputation for calmness in stressful situations but this stretched my equability and was in danger of destroying my record of dealing with such situations in a calm and rational manner. However, my inner-self prevailed and after a telephone call to the manager of the removal company in Jersey, albeit a tense but controlled conversation, I persuaded him that the vehicle had enough fuel capacity to reach us and in addition the supermarket chains with petrol stations had plenty of fuel for sale.

In the end our furniture arrived. I didn't say all of our furniture, because about a quarter of it was left behind in Jersey, so we had another three weeks to wait for that!! My fuse was burning quicker than normal but a substantial reimbursement from the removals company helped to ease the situation. We had already started the decoration and other tasks on the house before the furniture arrived so we busied ourselves throughout the Autumn, much as we had done on our house in Croatia during the winter and spring.

We had also set up our new computer, a laptop, which we were able to plug into a large monitor, printer, scanner, separate keyboard and mouse, but could be detached and taken with us to Croatia. One evening in February we were checking e-mails and saw a mysterious one from an address beginning with "Puntapet" and titled "Weather Report". It was from Robi and Erika!! What a joy to hear from our Croatian friends who we didn't expect to see until the spring. It turned out that they had made some folders in their little garage factory for a customer in Split but he did not have the money to pay for them (a common habit in Croatia it seemed) but he gave them a second hand computer in part payment. We received their first e-mail and so started our enjoyable correspondence with them through the magic of e-mail during the times we were away from Povlja.

This is what we received exactly as written:

"Finali message from us! I'm still learning so this letter could bee little bit confused because it is not easy to spell and vrite English vith two fingers. You knov Mr Mike don't do it proper vith pencil and even do I vith tastature and mouse! We got PC so now Youll bee fill vith mail. This is a first letter that I vrite and send so help me Good!

First address because I'm not sure do You get it vith letter. Here are everything same. Everiting is ok we all together are good, spreeng already come, we have fev Buras but we already forget them and veather is nice, and now I sound like proper English women talking about veather! We have good yob around New Year in vork shop but now is not so easy to collect moony but you know we aer used to it. Solgiers are still here, but comes only a few of them(7,10...) and they bring only Nepal solgiers which don't eat pizzas so evon is not ofthen hot. Everyone sends You regards and keep asking us when are You comming, I hope soon because I missed oure time vith You. Youre house is still standing, noone vork on next house and noone come to see vhats going on, You know from Supetar or Split. Robis cousen house still not finished. Punta look nice vith sunsets in this time of year and beach is little bit nicer after winters buras. Now I'm ocupated vith soiling, pc, garten so time passing quickly. I hope You and Youre family are OK, big kiss to everyone. Now I will finished and demanded ansver quickly as You can. Have a nice time, and have oure love Erika and Robi!!!!!

This cheered us no end knowing that we could keep in contact with our Croatian friends whilst in France. Erika's English was easy to understand in spite of the problem they all have with "w" and "v". We were really looking forward to returning to Povlja after receiving this message.

Driving around in France we noticed a lot of old blue Citroens with a black trim on the side, just like Robi's little car. He had had his for twenty years and drove everywhere in it seemingly without any faults. It was obviously a reliable model judging by the numbers around in the Correze, though like Robi's they were all looking old and careworn, but still going strong. Robi used his little car for everything, from collecting supplies for the restaurant and his other business, to delivering pizzas until late at night throughout the year. Whenever we saw one of them in France, we usually waved and said: 'There 's Robi!' The French drivers must have wondered who we were though we did get the occasional wave back.

It wasn't long before the end of March came along and we were packing for our next visit to our house in Povlja. We had decided to stay for two months this time and to try to let the house during the short tourist season of June, July and August to get some money back on our investment. We already had the house on a website for Povlja. Ivo, the South African boyfriend of Erika's sister, had constructed this. He had Croatian ancestry and often visited the Island, and on one of his visits he took photographs of our house and included it in the "accommodation" section. He also included, to my immense pleasure, photographs of some of my paintings of Povlja.

Our family and friends had also been spreading the word and handing out copies of a flyer I had put together on the computer. I was very proud of this though it had occupied a good deal of my evenings during the winter months as I was a complete self-taught novice on the computer and such things as "cutting and pasting" were learned the hard way. However, I was able to get instructions from our eleven-year old Jersey grandson, on the phone and on e-mail from time to time.

We shuttered up the French house and set off again for Croatia. Again we decided on the Frejus tunnel route and then through Italy to Ancona where we would get the Croatian ferry. The French motorways were as ever a pleasure to drive on but when we got on to the Italian autostradas we were again amongst the multitude of lorries, which pulled out with little or no notice into the fast lane, and the constant stream of very fast moving cars in the outer lane. On many stretches the road surface was badly potholed, which no doubt explained the many road works to make our journey even more painful! However, we had plenty of time to make stops to walk Rupert, have a coffee and to smoke my pipe, but mainly to make sure we got there safely. We did arrive unscathed in Ancona, except for the tension in our bodies after such a drive, but after we had bought our tickets, we had plenty of time to have a beer or two on the terrace of a harbour bar and watch the bustle of a busy port.

Boarding at 7pm was the same free for all we had experienced before but this time all we could do was laugh as cars jostled to get on the boat first. The ship was the "Dubrovnik", the sister ship of the "Marco Polo" and provided very much the same friendly, efficient service with a good inexpensive dinner to while away the time before retiring to our cabin. We were up and about on the deck at dawn to watch the sunrise and the ship pick its way through the many Islands before it reached Split. This was another world to us, of numerous islands, large and small (Croatia has over 1100, many of which are uninhabited), little fishing boats and small fishing villages dotted down the coast between the larger resorts. The stone houses with the terracotta roofs were a picture in the first rays of the early morning sun.

Disembarkation in Split was orderly and well controlled and surprisingly this time we had no problems with the customs official. It wasn't long before we were across on the ferry to Brac and driving across the quiet road to Povlja. The temptation to put my foot down to get there quickly was tempered by the knowledge that on the next bend may be a Croatian driver who was practising to drive in England, on the left hand side or just imitating the French. When we got to the top of the hill, this time we stopped to look down on Povlja and just doing that rid us of the tensions of the journey. Here we could relax; this was a place of no deadlines or pace of any kind; this was a place of "tomorrow will do"; and we were going to make the most of it.

Again the bush telegraph had worked as we drove through the village for Erika was at our gate to welcome us with her delightful smile and a twinkle in her eye.

"Ah, Miss March, Mr Mike, you get here safe. Ven you unpack you come have lunch, ve have a lot to tell you".

Then Robi appeared out of his garage workshop with his Peter Sellars' comic toothy smile. 'Hey neighbours, welcome back!'

It was a sunny mild day and Erika had opened our house to air. The shutters on the seaward side were covered in salt from the winter and March Buras, but that would be easily washed off, otherwise everything was all right. Rupert set to work peeing in all his strategic points in the garden to let the cats know that he was back and we busied ourselves unpacking.

We went up to Erika and Robi for a glass of red wine made by one of his friends to hear their news. Erica had already told us when we were in France that Robi had had an operation to remove a cancerous mole on his back. He was still receiving treatment and was trying to keep to a special diet; we had brought a load of information with us from trawling the internet on this particular cancer and the diet required. He had to keep off meat and had to eat vegetables so Erika had started a little vegetable garden which would help to boost the vegetables they received from her father's garden in the village. To help, we had brought a selection of seeds from France. The main problem for them though was that they had to pay for the treatment because Robi was deemed to have less than a fifty percent chance of recovering. The treatment was expensive and it was going to be hard for them to pay. Robi's mother and father had moved to a small apartment and rented out their house in Split to help raise the money.

Their main plan though was to close the restaurant. Apart from it being too much work for Robi, coupled with his share in a bar in Selca and his budding folder business, it barely brought in enough money to last them through the year. They were converting the restaurant into a small apartment, where they would live, and they would let their house out to tourists. There were many more tourists coming to Povlja now and the previous summer there was a shortage of accommodation. They would make much more this way, with far less work, no staff to worry about, and the chance to develop their little business based in the garage. This little enterprise had already improved and they were employing a girl full time on their little assembly line.

'Is Vedran still working for you in the garage?' I asked.

They laughed. 'No, Vedran vork in Zadar with brother on building site. He vas great entertainment but not suited to our vork!' said Robi.

We were a little sad that one of the "characters" had gone. Vedran's banter, jokes and "Hey neighbours, you vant a beer?" would be missed by us. We would also miss that delightful laughter from Kate and the many meals and chats with their friends in the restaurant. However, they would still be doing pizza takeaways so we said that we wanted a regular Saturday night order over the garden wall.

'Your usual?' laughed Erika.

'Yes, put everything you've got on it!' exclaimed March.

Erica served up lunch, which started with a lovely

vegetable soup and great hunks of brown and white bread. This was followed by fish, a pink colour rather like our Gurnard, which had been baked in the oven with olive oil. With this she served potatoes and a type of spinach cooked in garlic, mixed together in a bowl.

There was also finely cut white cabbage dressed in a local wine vinegar and seasoned heavily with salt and pepper, plus finely sliced large spring onions, seasoned with salt and marinated in the fridge in olive oil; the olive oil has a reaction with the onions which makes them taste superb.

Washed down with more glasses of Robi's friends wine we were in a happy mood. Happy to be back, and happy that Robi was seemingly well and his usual amusing self. After such a superb lunch we were also happy to indulge in the continental habit of the afternoon siesta.

We told Robi that we had seen many cars in France just like his and that we always waved. He was most amused but then went on to tell us that he had had a run-in with the police a few weeks before. He had been on his way to Supetar to deliver an order to be taken on the ferry to Split (this was quite common practise, you could put anything for delivery to Split next to the ramp on the ferry for someone to collect at the other end, at no charge). About half way there he was stopped by the police for speeding; Robi always drove everywhere at great speed. They demanded a fine of 200 kunas (about £18) but Robi responded: ' I have no money!'

'You must pay the fine', insisted the policeman.

'I have no money, shoot me!!' said Robi in ernest.

The policeman, amazingly, grinned and sent Robi on his way with only a caution. Robi said that the police would not normally have been as soft as that.

We quickly settled into the Povlja routine; walks to the village in the mornings to get the groceries and bread; chats with friends on the quay and a coffee in one of the cafes. Some days we would go to Selca for a change to say hello to the little hardware man and usually buy some teak stain for the shutters, window frames and doors, which we painted regularly to stop them from deteriorating in the Buras. He was always cheerful and pleased to see us but apart from stain he rarely had what we were looking for, but he always got it for us within a couple of days.

There was also a new grocer's shop in Povlja. Erika's "Best Man" at their wedding (Robi had a best man too), a cheerful friendly young man who we had often met in their house and restaurant, had opened a small shop next to the Dutch restaurant. This would rival the only other store, which many of the villagers didn't like so he felt he had a chance of making a living, particularly with the increasing number of tourists now taking the apartments. So long as they weren't Czechs, who brought their own food, he would probably do well. However things are not easy for young entrepreneurs in Croatia. His suppliers were very cagey about him and would not give him any credit at all, not even one month, so he had always to pay cash on delivery. Nevertheless he was making a go of it.

We met the Dutch couple one day when we had a

beer in their restaurant, which they were only running as a bar out of season. They had done quite well in the previous summer and reasonably well in the bar during the winter, particularly with the British soldiers. They were however bemoaning the problems foreigners have in starting businesses in Croatia. Apparently, the red tape was a nightmare, and they had to apply for work permits every year. Taxes on businesses were high, something Robi had previously said, so they were not as optimistic as they were the previous year. Their plans to open a water-sports centre and restaurant at the Punta were also seemingly stagnating in officialdom, which had been going on for over three years.

The sea was not warm enough for swimming yet, although it was still warmer than the sea in Jersey and the UK during their summer. We had been spoiled with the sea temperature of the previous summer of 28 degrees centigrade so we were not tempted, chickens that we were by the crystal clear blue water. So we busied ourselves with our crafts. I dashed off a few canvasses of the area and March busied herself with a large fabric picture of a flowering cactus we had. Whilst engrossed in our crafts one April morning, March came up with one of her ideas, which I always cringe at because it usually meant a lot of graft for me!

'How many paintings have you got here of Povlja?' she asked innocently.

'About sixteen at the last count,' I said hesitantly.

'Then you must hold an exhibition here,' she announced.

'Nobody is going to buy paintings here,' I squeaked. ' They don't have the money.'

'We won't do it for the money, we will do for the village as a bit of interest for them,' said March confidently.

'Where on earth can we hold it,' I bleated.

'Tonko will find somewhere, he's the head of tourism,' said March in full swing.

That was it, we were going to have a painting exhibition, so I knew what I would be doing for the next few days!!

Chapter 11

Art Exhibition and Canapes

We sought out Tonko at his favourite bar where he was playing cards with his usual chums, which often included Mr Boxer and Mr Lino. He leaped up from the table as he always did when we went into the bar and shook us warmly by the hand.

'Wie gehts, alles ok?'

'Sehr gut, danke.' We replied, as he ushered us to another table, where we ordered beers. We chatted away in German, which was occasionally interspersed with a bit of English when he recalled certain words, but we got on well as usual in spite of not having spoken German a great deal for many years except for ordering beers and food on our Austrian skiing holidays. His daughter and little grandchild, who lived in Vienna were arriving shortly for a short holiday so we were invited for an evening up at his house above the village.

We broached the subject of my intended painting exhibition and he was delighted. He doubted that I would sell any paintings as the wealthier tourists were not around in the spring, but I said that I wanted to do it as a bit of interest for the locals. He had a good idea for the venue. The Croatian post office had built a grand new stone post office at the end of the harbour. It was a magnificent building, far too big for the one girl who normally ran the service, but nevertheless a lovely stone structure showing off the Croatian stone craft at its best. It had been finished the previous summer and there had been a big ceremony with a band and lots of dignitaries from both the post office and Croatian telecoms who had shared the cost as they used part of the building. However, Tonko told us, there was a dispute between the two organisations as to the share of the costs of running the place so the building was not open for business! He knew one of the directors of the post office in Split so he said he would ask if we could use it.

The following week we went up to Tonko's house to meet his daughter and grandchild. Tonko's wife Dalmina welcomed us and seated us on their downstairs terrace which was covered in vines and had bougainvillea, not yet in flower, growing up the walls. It was a lovely sunny evening and their view across the harbour and across to the mainland with the sea stretching out before us was stunning. The warm almost apricot reflected glow of the limestone mountains on the mainland was sandwiched between the rich blue sea and a cloudless clear blue sky. The terracotta rooftops of Povlja stretched out beneath them down to the harbour where the little fishing boats were setting out for their evening fishing. They had a truly idyllic spot to live.

Tonko had good news that we could use the post office and he would get hold of the keys. We then had a delightful meal which started with mussels cooked very similarly to the French "moule marinere" and continued with grilled lamb from their outside BBQ. All this was washed down with Tonko's own excellent red wine and with the coffee, made the Turkish way, his own slivovic. This tasted a little bit like the Italian grappa but with a little extra "kick". We didn't have to speak German all evening as his daughter, a lovely cheerful girl, spoke excellent English. However I had noticed on many previous occasions that our German improved amazingly with the more wine we consumed so it wasn't too much of a strain on the old grey matter. After an entertaining evening, and full of good cheer, we walked back to the Punta along the harbour with the twinkling lights reflected in the water, and discussed what arrangements we would have to make for the exhibition.

We had arranged with Tonko to hold the exhibition in the first week of May so we had a couple of weeks to get things organised. We decided to have an opening party and would then have the paintings on display for three mornings after the opening. I set to work to make the posters we would need; one in each shop, one in the new post office and one in the old post office. I did these free-hand and painted a little water colour on each one.

We thought we would have wine and orange juice for drinks and would also provide some nibbles or canapés of some sort. This proved to be the most difficult of our tasks as the local shops, we soon discovered, didn't have the necessary ingredients for canapés. Suzy came to the rescue when she said that a new supermarket had opened in Supetar and that they would almost certainly have what we wanted.

So off we went to explore. We found plain biscuits, meat and fish pastes, stuffed olives, bottled anchovies and soft cheese, so we had the ingredients to make a spread. It would have been nice if we had found some cocktail sausages and vol-au-vents but that was not to be. March also said she would make some quiches, which we could slice into manageable handfuls and Erika volunteered to do some small pizzas.

I also set to work to paint another couple of local seascapes to fill up the large space in the new post office. Whenever we went into the village, as the date of the exhibition approached, we were often approached by various locals to say that they were really looking forward to it. The day before Erika came with us to clean up the post office as it still had quite a bit of builder's dust about on the polished stone and on the large arch shaped windows. We also took all my paintings and arranged them as best we could on the furniture and counters. We had quite a laugh doing this as Erika is always full of fun.

So the great day arrived and we were both up early making the canapés and arranging them onto large plates, which Erika had loaned us. Then as it neared the time for us to go down to open the post office we had a minor disaster. Some of the biscuits we had used for the canapés had gone a bit soft, so we hurriedly put them into the fan oven to dry out in the remaining time available. Fortunately it worked so off we drove with the car loaded.

The exhibition was timed to open at 1030 am and would go on to about 1230. We were there at about 10am to set out the food and for me to open the bottles of wine. Then another minor disaster when I knocked over three bottles of red wine which went all over the polished stone floor which seemed to soak it all up like a sponge. This was the magnificent cream stone floor of the new post office, soiled before it opened by a clumsy Englishman. I then went into panic mode but fortunately Tonko was arriving and immediately shot off to borrow a mop from the nearest bar. We had only just managed to clean it up by the time the first people arrived. But there was still an ominous red stain which we would have to tackle later. I was feeling pretty embarrassed about this and wondered whether Tonko felt we had already been on the bottle!

When about twenty people had gathered in the post office Tonko made a speech about me. As it was in Croatian I had no idea what he was saying. I then made a short speech in English and Erika followed with the translation she had made from my notes I had made the day before. I said how much I loved Povlja and how I had first seen the village from the road above and knew I must paint that scene. I waxed lyrical about the colour of the sea and the stunning sunsets mainly to blank faces of the older ones, who didn't speak English, but to pleasure on the faces of those who did.

Erika was a little nervous but gave the translation

confidently and in a strong voice to lots of oohs and aahs from the assembly, which was swelling by the minute. It became apparent that Erika had taken my modest little speech and embellished it somewhat as it was much longer than mine! However from the smiling faces it all went down well so we passed around the drinks and canapés whilst the guests viewed the paintings. They were delighted to see on canvas the views they all knew well. There also seemed to be arguments about who's boat was who's in the harbour scenes. One old chap I saw was standing in front of a painting I had done of a single boat moored stern on to the harbour wall with the bow anchored out to sea. I was particularly proud of this one and how I had managed to paint the clear water and the shadow of the boat on the stones beneath, but he stood there shaking his head. Alarmed I took Erika over to find out what was wrong and Erika translated the old man's reply: ' I like the painting but you have painted the boat facing the wrong way.' He grinned and then lectured me on how boats should be moored. I didn't argue and merely apologised for my ignorance, but I had a photograph of the boat I had taken whilst painting the picture, so perhaps the owner had preferred it that way.

When they had all looked intently at all the pictures they stood in groups chatting in the way they always did, loudly and cheerfully, so it all developed into a good party.

Apart from lots of complements on my paintings to which I muttered 'I do my best', we had a tremendous complement about the canapés. One lady said that everyone was most impressed and most had never seen such nibbles before and that they were as artistic and colourful as the paintings!

People came and went during the two hours and at the end all the food was gone and most of the wine; we had about thirty litres at the start and it certainly helped to increase the noise level and general bonhomie. We reckoned that we had had over sixty people for the exhibition so we were well pleased. Everyone shook us warmly by the hand when they left and one old chap said that nobody had ever done anything like that for them before.

That afternoon we cleaned up with Erika's assistance and tackled the red stain on the floor. We were determined to get it off as we did not want to get Tonko into trouble with the post office, although he was not particularly concerned, or the post office to think the English were an untidy lot of alcoholics, who spilt more than they drank. Most of the cleaning materials we tried would not shift the stain so we then tried the old faithful Domestos, which thankfully did the trick. Feeling good at the success of the exhibition and getting the wine stain removed, we retired to our terrace to have a well-earned glass of wine with Erika who related the various favourable comments she had heard at the exhibition. All in all we felt pretty happy, and deciding that I didn't want to cook that evening we ordered two of Erika's delicious takeaway pizzas.

*

During the winter another house had been built at the Punta. We were told that it belonged to Americans but so far we had not seen them. The house was almost completed and the weekend after my exhibition the Americans appeared. They certainly set to work on their garden, removing the scrub and the many large stones. It was pretty hot and they kept at it most of the day, putting us to shame as we were having a relaxing weekend free from jobs.

Towards the end of the afternoon I went over to say hallo and invite them for a drink. I met Hank as he was wheeling a barrow-load of cuttings to the tip. He was tall, slim and rugged looking with a cigarette hanging from his lip in the Bogart fashion and he spoke slowly in a southern drawl with a voice like gravel. I could just imagine him in a western movie running a bar in Tombstone. He was pleased about the invitation and said they would be around shortly when they had washed up.

Hank and his wife Maive duly arrived and we settled down on our terrace in the warmth of the evening. We stuck to our wine but they chose beer to quench their thirsts after a hard day in the sun. My stock of beer rapidly declined as a result but it certainly loosened their tongues. Mind you it doesn't take a lot to get Americans talking; most we have met on our travels will tell you their family history right down to shoe sizes without the slightest prompting; something the reticent English find quite foreign to their nature. They were good company and we learned that he was in their diplomatic corps with a job somewhere in Bosnia. They had been there for several years and had fell in love with the Dalmatian coast much the same as we had. He hadn't long to go before retirement and Povlja was where they wanted to be. During the course of the evening we had several text messages on our mobile from various children and friends in Jersey. This was far more than normal and I kept leaping up to pick up the mobile phone, which we had left in the living room.

The signal we had chosen on the mobile for text messages was morse code as it reminded me of old army days when it was still used as a backup means of communication. I could see that Hank was becoming increasingly interested in the morse code signal and my leaping off into the house for a few minutes each time. He then asked suspiciously: 'Is that a radio transmitter you have in there?'

'No, just our mobile', I said innocently.

'Do you mind if I use your John?' asked Hank.

'No, not at all, I'll show you', I said and led Hank through the living room and into the hall where I pointed out our Lavatory.

On the way Hank walked quite slowly and looked around the living room and the hallway with great interest and narrowed eyes. It was obvious that he didn't believe the mobile phone story and was looking for a radio transmitter. He was a fairly long time so he was either one of those who spend ages in lavatories or he was having a good look around the rest of the house! I was beginning to chuckle secretly about this and wondered whether Hank was CIA or something.

My son Mark had once told me that when he was a European Monitor during the Balkan war, he often worked with Americans who were all convinced that he and his British colleagues were all from the British Secret Intelligence Service! Hank obviously had the same idea about me.

It was midnight before we retired after a pleasant evening, my beer stock severely depleted, not that I minded, though Hank seemed non the worse for wear.

The next day Hank and Maive worked hard again on their garden but had to depart before 3pm to get the ferry to Makarska and then onward over the hill into Bosnia. They were going to be regular weekenders in Povlja so we looked forward to their company again. Hank and Maive would feel at home with RADEEEO BRAAACH as the local radio station, with its: 'MUSIC TO TAKE YOUR BREATHAWAY' and 'AN AMERICAN RADIO STATION IN YOUR TOWN' or 'MUSIC AND MORE' in that drawling voice a lot of American broadcasters have. But perhaps they would want to be away from all that. However the Punta was certainly getting an international flavour with English, Austrians and now Americans.

The weather was very warm and we had a strengthening wind from the south called the "Jugo", which means south in Croatian, hence Jugoslavia being the country of the southern slavs. The Jugo increased in strength, not quite Bura proportions but nevertheless quite strong and it went on for almost a week. March complained of nausea and giddiness and started to have headaches but at first we did not attribute it to the Jugo until Robi and Erika said they always suffered the same symptoms during Jugos. Often people become quite depressed and suicidal during this wind but thankfully we did not get those symptoms. I was lucky in not having any ill effects at all. I don't get seasickness either so that may have something to do with it.

The Jugo passed by the next weekend and we were invited to Robi and Erika's for lunch on the Saturday with her parents and "the people from Bol", as she called her sister and her husband Emir and their two little daughters. Instead of the people from Bol, March christened them the "Bolognese" much to everyone's amusement but the nickname stuck. Saturday lunches were a regular feature for Erika's family at her house and we were pleased to be invited because they were all such a friendly, happy and jolly crowd. Lunch was always excellent as Erika often grilled or baked fresh fish, which had been caught that morning. One of their friends was Petar, the son of the man who owned the big fishing boat "the Povlja" and Petar would pop around with fish for them when the boat docked after a nights fishing off Hvar, a neighbouring island where the fish were more plentiful. They loved March's apple pies so whenever we were invited we always took one. One thing we noticed at these lunches was that they all put water into the red or "black" wine as they called it. I personally hate any water in red wine no matter how strong they claimed it to be!

That lunch Robi told us that he had had trouble with the tax authorities.

'The tax man punish me.' Robi exclaimed.

He had been doing the accounts for the last year they had run the restaurant and had also sent off his completed tax return. The taxman was not happy with Robi's handwriting on the tax return so had fined him quite a large sum in punishment! March and I were amazed but realised that the old communist attitude was probably still around in the civil administration.

As the weather was so good we decided to have a dinner party the following week. We had an ulterior motive in that Suzy and Simon, the English reservist sailing instructor at the army centre based in the hotel, were now an entity and were living in a house next to her parents and grandmother. We had often chatted to Simon as he had been in Povlja longer than we had because he had always managed to prolong his posting probably due to the army's shortage of sailing instructors. He had been running his own carpentry business in England before he had volunteered for this posting. He had therefore found a small workshop on the ground floor of a house on the quay in Povlja and was doing bits and pieces of carpentry in his spare time. He loved Povlja and wanted to stay after the army ever moved out or dispensed with his services, so he hoped to develop a little business before that happened.

We also invited Erika and Robi and another young couple who were their friends and had been regular visitors at our Saturday evenings in the restaurant during those first winter months. He was called Goran, a large jolly and intelligent young man who had developed his own small building business in Povlja after giving up his job in Split, but his work was all done on the "black" as was most building and construction work on the island. Both he and his wife, a bubbly blonde called Dinka, spoke excellent English so we had no language worries.

We sat outside on our terrace in the warm early evening. I had decided to cook a French-type four-course meal starting with roasted peppers in olive oil, anchovies, garlic and parsley. This was followed with coq au vin, mashed potatoes topped with a little cheese and put under the grill for a few minutes to form a lovely crisp topping and carrots cut into matchsticks and fried quickly in butter and chopped ginger. We then had some cheese we had bought from an old lady we had given a lift to. It was a bit like the French Cantal but amazingly twice the price!! We of course finished off the meal with apple pie and custard, which went down well with Simon, reminding him of England, but particularly with Goran. Like me he was a keen cook, something rare in Croatian households, and he really loved March's pastry and insisted she write down the recipe right away.

As the evening drew in we put on the outside lights and brought out candles, which helped to produce a very convivial atmosphere. We talked about everything, including politics and religion and consumed a great deal of red wine. Whilst on politics it was mentioned that on the news some English politician was in disgrace because of an affair with a married woman. I laughed and said that the French never worried about that sort of thing as all their politicians were having affairs, and according to our French friends, including Jacques Chirac himself.

Goran then said: 'Our politicians all have affairs but

we not worried. We more worried about them robbing the people!'

Whilst said as a joke it was an indication of how a lot of people felt about their politicians.

*

A couple of days later we were in Selca getting some shopping when we saw Vedran sitting on a bench under a tree. As we walked towards him he recognised us and leaped up with a broad grin on his face.

'Hello Vedran!' I exclaimed.

'You remember my name,' he said with obvious pleasure. 'Hello neighbours', he said as he shook us both warmly by the hand.

He told us how he had been working on building sites in Sibenik on the coast, but mostly how he missed working up at Robi and Erika's in their little workshop. He also said how he had missed us and how we must all get together.

'You must come around for a drink and a chat, anytime.' I said.

'Ttenk you, I hev idea for new business'.

He then told us of a scheme he was hatching to start a business. He had decided that he would become an estate agent and sell properties to wealthy westerners, but he had no money to start up the business. We immediately realised that he viewed us as potential partners but we didn't encourage him further, as likeable as he was, we didn't view him as a good risk.

'You won't need much to start,' I said. 'All you need

is a mobile phone, a briefcase and a car, just like most of the other Croatian businessmen.'

He obviously realised that we were not biting so he moved on to other topics of conversation such as the weather etc. He said that he had to go but would come to Povlja to see us in a few days, but he did not appear.

That week March said one morning: 'We have been here almost two years and you havn't taken me to Dubrovnik!' What more could I say to that than: 'Ok, why don't we go next week. The weather is lovely and there won't be so many tourists in mid-May, hopefully.'

I had been to Dubrovnik with my son Mark back in 1996 not long after the Balkan war had ended. We had seen the damage the Serb shells had done to that beautiful historic city. They had patched up a lot of the damage from over 2000 artillery, tank and mortar shells but the evidence was there for all to see. It would be interesting to see how they had repaired what was one of the world's most outstanding cities but also to lap up the shear beauty and history of the place.

Chapter 12

Dubrovnik

We had chosen the following Monday for our three-day trip to Dubrovnik. Our car was loaded so that when the alarm went off at "Sparrow's fart", as we used to say in the army, all we had to do was to snatch a little breakfast and drive the fifteen minutes to Sumartin, to catch the six am ferry to Makarska on the coast.

It was still dark as we arrived early at this little fishing port to get into line for the ferry. There were a couple of lorries and a handful of cars with their drivers standing around chatting in the dim lights of the harbour; like most things in Croatia this was yet another social event. A gaggle of schoolchildren laughed and fooled around under a street lamp by the ferry as they waited for their bus.

At last the lights were turned on the ferry, an old tub which looked more like a WW2 tank landing craft than a more modern means of transport, and we were signalled forward to drive onto the ferry. We had to manoeuvre so that we could back onto it as it only had the one door. As we were doing this, the school-bus arrived and proceeded to force its way through the ferry traffic to pick up the children. Boarding of the ferry was stopped whilst this traffic jam was sorted out in the tight space at the end of the ferry ramp. Why another pick up point could not have been selected for the schoolchildren or a different time arranged was beyond us, but we were used to this sort of chaos now and just laughed. Two years before we would both have been cursing and raging at the situation. We were obviously eventually going to get onto the ferry so why worry! Relax!

Having boarded the ferry we settled into the little lounge and the ferry cast off, bound on its one-hour journey to Makarska. It was still just dark as we left but about half way across we could see through the windows that the sunrise was appearing over the mountains on the coast and the wonderful apricot glow was lighting up the slopes and reflecting on the dark blue calm sea. By now the lounge, with its little bar serving coffee, beer and schnapps to the travellers was full of cigarette smoke (most Croatians seem to smoke), so we decided to watch the continuing sunrise from the upper deck.

We took photographs of this wonderful scene of the sea, mountains and the islands lit up in the morning glow; this was a picture I would have to paint as I had not experienced a sunrise like it. We could now see the many little fishing boats and some larger ones with their derricks hauling in the nets as we approached the natural harbour of Makarska.

Surprisingly Makarska was a bustle of activity as we

drove off the ferry. Shops and cafes were open but we were not stopping as it was a good three hours drive down the coast to Dubrovnik. This proved to be a wonderful experience in itself. It was reminiscent of the coastal drive from Sorrento to Positano on the Italian coast but here we had the added beauty of the many Islands, large and small, dotted along the coast. The only disconcerting thing was that the road was quite high up above the sea and in many places there were no roadside barriers. I think March, who was closest to the edge, had her eyes firmly closed on several bends.

I was certainly encouraged to drive slowly on several occasions, with 'Mike! You are too near the edge!' or 'Slow down!'

Nevertheless the view was stunning. With only a short stop for coffee and buns at a little café overlooking the sea, we were making good time. As we left the café we noticed a sign with farewell messages in several languages:

"Merci - au revoir"

"Danke - auf wiedersehen" etc

But the English version made us laugh:

"Tenks - goodbye"

Eventually we came to a large flat agricultural plain as the road took us a little way inland. The valley was full of a variety of crops but by far the most were olive groves and acres of orange trees. Soon the sides of the road on both sides were inundated with little stalls selling big bags of oranges and bottles of local schnapps.

We stopped to buy a large bag of oranges, about £2

for a 5 kilo bag, and sampled a couple. Easy to peal rather like Clementines, they were sweet and juicy, and an excellent mid-morning treat.

During the trip along the coast we came to a border post to go through a short stretch Bosnia, which was given part of the coast as an outlet to the sea, under the Datona agreement at the end of the Balkan war. On seeing the colour of our EU style passports we were waved through without a stop, though we noticed that other nationalities, mainly Czechs, were being questioned.

It doesn't take long to drive through this short bit of Bosnia- Herzegovina. There are a few villages on the road and all of them are packed with shops selling food, clothing and household goods at much lower prices than Croatia, due to the zero Vat. It is a favourite stop for Croatians to stock up on food and many items they cannot get in their own shops so the car parks of all the shops were pretty full.

From Makarska driving south to Dubrovnik, Croatia gets narrower and narrower, rather like driving into a wedge with only the one main road going south. There had been quite a few lorries along the road but we were not worried as we were taking it easy and enjoying the scenery. But after the short bit of Bosnia-Herzegovina the lorries veered off onto the main road to Sarajevo so the rest of the drive was pretty quiet. Down the coast there were many little resorts with hotels, apartments and restaurants but we noticed that many of these were closed in May. Though some of the little ports had ferries which plied regular traffic to the islands.

We arrived in Dubrovnik at 11am and soon found our hotel not far from the old city. The hotel was similar to the hotels at Plitvica; utilitarian and cavernous, but clean. The receptionist was friendly and spoke good English but she was not sure our dog Rupert was allowed in the hotel. She went off to consult the duty manager who appeared looking doubtful.

'He is only a little dog and is very well behaved,' said March.

'Shall I get him for you to see,' she continued.

March duly went to the car without waiting for a reply and brought Rupert into the foyer. All the receptionists cooed over him and he responded with his usual Westie charm and friendliness, his tail wagging and revolving like a windmill.

Confronted with this the manager nodded. 'Ok, he stay.'

Unlike France we had found on several occasions that dogs in Croatia were not welcome in hotels, restaurants and in many of the rooms on the ferries. In France we had taken Rupert everywhere so we found the Croatian attitude to dogs rather strange.

We quickly offloaded our baggage and set off on foot to the old city, which we were assured was only a twenty-minute walk. It was already hot and sunny and with Rupert in tow we strolled through the outskirts following the signs to the city centre. However after twenty minutes we seemed to be still a long way off and March was getting a little frustrated with my navigation. She was always pretty rude about one of my favourite remarks of: 'It's just around the corner.' It was also into lunchtime and when March is hungry I always get a hard time. Fortunately around the next corner we came across the ancient massive ramparts, which surround the old city. We found one of the gates across a timber bridge spanning the ravine below the ramparts on the landward side of the city and were soon strolling down the main thoroughfare, which was thronging with people.

The initial impression of Dubrovnik is of an ancient city steeped in history. The architecture is Venetian and many of the buildings are very old and very grand. It has obviously had a rich past and a magnificent cultural heritage. It is well preserved and I could see no signs of the damage I had seen in 1996 from the Serb bombardment within the city walls but outside we had noticed the telltale "splat" of a mortar or artillery shells in some of the pavements and roads.

Although the city had been conquered six times in its history, it had suffered destruction only twice: in an earthquake in 1667 and, as the guide-book said, in the invasion of modern-day Balkan barbarians in 1991!

The streets, houses and shops were not tainted with the paraphernalia of signs and advertising and other present day clutter which ruin many western ancient cities. Apart from the dress of the people one could be strolling down a seventeenth century street.

The main thoroughfare was strewn with outdoor cafes with customers enjoying the sun and people-watching. The grey paving stones had a sheen which gave the appearance of wetness but in fact was a smooth polished effect brought about by the feet of thousands of people over the centuries.

We were soon accosted by a pretty young girl who thrust a leaflet in my hand with details of a restaurant which she insisted had excellent food, so we decided to give it a try. She directed us up a steep set of stone steps to a street which was lined with numerous small restaurants with tables and parasols on the narrow street, between tall Italian-looking houses. Here the sun only penetrated to the top storeys leaving the restaurants in the welcome shade of the houses.

The waiter noticed straight away that we were English and chatted to us as he settled us into our table and handed out menus. We ordered a carafe of red wine and scanned the list of food on offer. We are not big lunch eaters so we were only interested in one course; March settled for spaghetti Bolognese and I a seafood risotto. The wine was good and we enjoyed watching the passing tourists being chatted up by the waiters to sit down and have a meal in their restaurant. We were amazed at how many languages some of them spoke as they conversed freely in Italian, German and English who seemed to make up most of the passing trade. One couple of tourists were tackled in all three languages as a waiter tried to identify their nationality but when they replied in Spanish, probably hoping they were safe to escape, he spoke to them in what seemed to be fluent Spanish. What a star!

Our food arrived and was good, but nothing special to recommend to a good food guide. As we ate our meal we were accompanied by some rather pleasant classical violin music drifting from a third floor window with an old balcony where the daily washing was drying. Much better than the wallpaper music you get in English restaurants. Our waiter brought us both a glass of local brandy saying: 'Compliments of ze ouse, you come again, no.' All in all it was a very enjoyable occasion and set us up for more explorations of the city.

After diving down numerous little alleyways and narrow streets all filled with cafes, shops and restaurants in the heat of the day we were pleased to stumble upon an old monastery which had a central quadrangle surrounded by a magnificent arched cloisters which were cool and quiet. We sat on a bench in the quadrangle amongst lush green trees and bushes with not even the sound of a bird to disturb us. Whilst enjoying the peace it was difficult to believe that this was in the middle of a busy thriving city. Meditation over, and much cooler than an ice cream could have achieved, we were back into the bustle of polished streets, but it was time to indulge in one of our favourite sports of people watching from some suitable café. Sipping our cold Croatian beer we noticed how many different nationalities there were and of all ages too.

Before we heard the voices of the passers-by we always tried to guess the nationalities, and after many years of doing this we are mostly right in our guesswork. We usually agree, but that afternoon March cast her eyes over a young family, with three small children and one on the way, all rather scruffily dressed and said: 'English'.

'Definitely not,' I argued. 'They look Dutch or Danish to me.'

'No, they are English, just look at the designer scruffiness!'

She was right too. They sat down at a table near to us in a scramble of table and seat re –arranging, surrounded by a clutter of pushchairs and toys and ordered in Essex type accents a variety of drinks and ice creams. Anyway we gave them full marks for being so adventurous with such a young family. Croatia must also be catching on with the English.

Back at the hotel after a much needed shower we enquired about a suitable restaurant and were delighted that we only had to walk next door to a little bistro which had Balkan, Italian and French cuisine. The waitress was very friendly and spoke good English so we were able to quiz her on places to visit the next day.

We had a good meal starting with a local fish soup, not quite up to French style but nevertheless tasty. March then had a steak au poivre and I had an unpronounceable dish of several meats, which the waitress said was a sort of mixed grill. With this we had chips, a great treat as we hadn't had any for ages, and some overcooked vegetables. It was not a gastronomic feast but we enjoyed it along with the local red wine, which was as good as most of the red wine I have tasted in Europe. Croatia is not the place for gastronomic tourists. The food is in general wholesome but unimaginative, though we have never had any really bad food there. However, one good thing about it, it is very cheap and there is always plenty of it for the healthy appetite, or unhealthy appetite, whichever way you look at it.

The next morning we were up early and quickly down to a continental style breakfast with the most watered down orange juice I have ever tasted. Strange considering that just up the coast they have more cheap oranges than you could shake a stick at. The coffee tasted a bit ersatz too but we were keen to get into the city. This time we decided to drive and get to one of the car parks below the city walls and luckily got one of the few remaining places. It was sunny but not yet too hot so we opted for a walk on the huge ramparts surrounding the city. We climbed up and up the steep steps to the top of the walls.

I had never seen a city or castle wall quite so high and at the top our legs were screeching with pain rather like after a long downhill schuss when skiing. Poor little Rupert with his short legs gave up half way and refused to go any further so I had to carry him. Nevertheless it was well worth it as the views of the city enclosed below and the clear blue sea were magnificent. The walls in places have quite narrow walkways with heart-in-the-mouth drops to look down but in most places it is quite wide and the fortifications include numerous large turrets.

With the terracotta roofs on one side and a steep drop to the sea on the other we made our way along the seaward side of the ramparts. We only had one short stop for a well-earned beer at a small café on the wall but by lunchtime we had only traversed half of the walls. We had reached the famous harbour to which we descended down some more steep steps. Little boats were bobbing about on their moorings and tourists were still queuing for boat trips to the islands but we didn't dally as by now our stomachs were telling us in no uncertain terms that a nosebag was required.

Turning through the main city gate arch towards the main thoroughfare we were suddenly confronted by a multitude of small people. I'm talking small here as I am about six feet and I was towering over them all. We were quite stunned and both stopped abruptly. Regaining our consciousness we realised that they were all Japanese, most of whom in dark suits seemed to be gathered around a pretty little woman in a diaphanous dress. Still in the stationary position and staring at this small throng with open mouths, probably looking quite stupid, they passed by with one or two of the small Ninja type warriors in dark suits giving us some suspicious looks. We later discovered that it was a visit from a member of the Japanese Royal Family.

We decided not to run the gauntlet of "restaurant alley", where we had eaten the day before, due to the constant canvassing of the waiters saying: 'Pleeze take seat, our food werry excellent. You vant seafood, steaks, pleeze sit here.' Amusing, but a bit tedious after passing two or three restaurants in line abreast.

We settled for a small restaurant on its own down a little alleyway and sat outside where, although we were out of the sunlight, it was still very warm. A woman in her sixties, whom we christened "Mrs Miggins", delivered the menu and said: ' Werry good food, my son he cook,' baring her nicotine stained and slightly rotten teeth in a "Mrs Miggins-style" toothy grin.

'Viz food you have free aperitif and glass of vine, you like?'

'Dobro', I said trying to impress, and she gave us another show of her teeth and disappeared into what appeared to be a sort of "Black hole of Calcutta", which nevertheless seemed to be issuing rather pleasant gastronomic smells.

Erica and Robi had said that we had to try the "Black risotto" whilst we were here so we opted for that, although March did have reservations.

It duly arrived with another toothy grin from the Miggins woman, steaming platefuls of black rice and diced cuttlefish (the black appearance coming from the ink of the fish). It looked pretty inedible, due to its blackness but it tasted really delicious. They say that food should look good on a plate, colourful and artistically presented, but this was a heap of black mess and didn't look the least appetising. But it showed how the eye could deceive as we really enjoyed the dish. It was filling too.

One thing we had to do was to see the view of the city from the outside, which all the holiday brochures show. It is a view taken from the coast just to the south and shows the harbour with the massive tower to the left and the ramparts around the old city topped with its terracotta roofs giving a brilliant splash of colour in the sunlight. The drive was stunning, climbing up to the top of some very steep cliffs, which provided the desired view.

The brilliant sun shone down on the ultramarine blue of the Adriatic sea which glittered like diamonds around the city ramparts glistening almost a brilliant white. Away to the north the many islands provided contrasting colours of green trees and creamy stone and the many boats both large and small busied themselves between the islands. This was picture postcard stuff and we were part of it, soaking it all up.

A little further along the coast we came across a derelict hotel, which had been damaged during the Balkan war and from where some of the tanks and artillery had shelled the city in 1991. It was an eerie reminder of what had been so we didn't linger long. As we were leaving in the morning we went back into the city for one last stroll around its charming streets. After another good meal that night in a nearby restaurant followed by some beers and kruscovacs (a bit like a strong cough medicine on ice but tasty) on the hotel terrace we were ready for a good nights sleep.

We had a leisurely start to the day as we planned to lunch in either Ston or Mali Ston just up the coast about an hours drive from Dubrovnik. We had all day to get to Makarska for the ferry so we were going to take it easy, just as we liked it.

Ston is on the coast and has a thriving mussel and oyster farming industry but also boasts some pretty good seafood restaurants, which are popular with the international agencies and diplomatic corps in Bosnia. It is not a long drive for them so lunch in Ston is a regular event particularly as they have pretty fat salaries and expense accounts. They often fill up the restaurants there; middle aged men with their young Bosnian female interpreters in tow.

'I bet their wives would be livid if they knew what their husbands were up to', said March caustically.

'I'd put salt on your tail if it were you!'

'Yes Darling', I said meekly. Best to keep quiet when March is in full flow!

Mind you the female interpreters were rather attractive so you could see why the chaps were straying a little, or perhaps a lot.

We found a little restaurant in the back streets of Ston, which is on the Peljesac peninsular where one of our favourite wines is made. Above Ston is a steep hill with a medieval fortress surrounded by a wall, which must run for miles up and down the steep slopes and around the hill.

There were some tourists around, including some Parisians, who questioned us about our French number plate. They were from a Cunard cruise ship which had docked in Dubrovnik and were having a days sightseeing. We were amazed to see the French in Croatia as they are not great travellers in Europe, preferring to take their holidays in France. They were certainly the first French we had ever encountered there and we were pleased they liked what they had seen.

Naturally we opted for seafood for lunch. March had langoustines in garlic butter and I had grilled Baby squid in olive oil and garlic. With a little salad and bread to mop up the remaining juices we had a meal to remember.

We couldn't linger too long as we had to get to the ferry, so reluctantly we dragged ourselves away. We knew we would return there as we wanted to explore the Peljesac peninsular and cross from there on a short ferry trip to Korcula (pronounced Korchula) where Marco Polo's house is and where Fitzroy Maclean, the British military advisor to Tito during the war had lived.

Waiting for the ferry in a little café under the palms on the harbour in Makarska, we overheard an elderly couple on the next table speaking English so we engaged them in conversation.

'Enjoying your holiday?' asked the old boy.

'Oh we live here', I replied. 'We have a house on Brac just over there'. I continued proudly.

'We live here too. We have lived in Makarska for over fourteen years'.

'Wow', I said. 'We thought we were the pioneers here and we have only been here for two years'.

Chapter 13

More Weather Reports from Erica

Back in Povlja, March made the suggestion that we should be giving something back to the community. We had received so much help and had been made so welcome, plus we were constantly being given home made wine, olive oil and schnapps, so we had to find a way to do something in return. An idea sprang to March from learning that Erika had for some time been giving English lessons to some of the children in the village.

The children learned basic English at school but the lessons were limited and to get a good grounding the parents had to pay for extra tuition, something which many could not afford. Erika had some American-English children's books but was unhappy that the children were not learning proper English. March had managed to have a small number of books posted out from Jersey so decided to start Saturday afternoon classes free of charge with Erika's help. Suzy offered to do a poster in Croatian on Simon's computer announcing the lessons and put them up in the post office, the local store and the village hall.

The first Saturday came along and we had two girls and two boys all around eight to ten years. They already had some English so March who was to take the classes, with me in reserve, set them off reading aloud one by one, around our stone table on the patio on a lovely sunny afternoon. One of the boys, Alan, was very keen and quite good at reading and understood most of the words. The girls were good too but one of the boys was struggling. Their main problem was pronunciation, because apart from listening to English music, or watching "Ello Ello" on TV with those funny French accents, they had never spoken to English people before.

Very was pronounced werry, and for village it was willage (we had noticed Erika saying this so we now always said willage!).

There was also the usual problem, which continentals have of not being able to pronounce the th in the etc – it was always ze, zis or zat or de, dis or dat. Quite useful for us English in past wars, as most spies were soon rounded up quite quickly. 'Vich is de vay to de railvay station?' Said to even the dimmest would in 1942 in the heart of England result in an immediate arrest or call for the police!

So we had to concentrate on them to get their pronunciation right. We all had great fun teaching them to put their tongues between their teeth and "thissing" like a snake. Also to put their top teeth over their bottom lips to get the v's. This all helped to relieve a little bit of tension, which had built up as they were all excessively competitive. We didn't want our sessions to be too serious as we might lose the weaker ones. We wanted it all to be fun whilst improving their English. Getting them to do their little pronunciation exercises had us all rolling around in laughter particularly over the amount of spray coming out of their mouths when they tried their th's, so we were beginning to achieve our aim. They did about an hour of reading and then we just chatted around the table about the things they were interested in. At least they were hearing English people speaking and pronouncing the language.

The next Saturday we had six. One little girl turned up with some chocolates and a boy with a bottle of home made olive oil. Their parents were obviously pleased or perhaps glad to get rid of them for a couple of hours. We used the same format of reading aloud first and then chatting. March took the four girls and I the boys. We had Croatian dictionaries so any words they didn't understand we would just look up or we would mime just like in a game of charades.

The boys and I had a great chat about football which was their main passion. They were well up on the English teams and players with David Beckham as one of their heroes. It was no wonder with all this fervour that a small country like Croatia had such a good international side. They were also keen on basketball and handball, but when I spoke about rugby they were a bit puzzled, so I had to make a fool of myself by demonstrating how the game was played which had them laughing. I didn't even dare to mention cricket as it would be like explaining it to a bunch of Martians. A lot of English people don't understand the game anyway!

Ever since we had been in Povlja we had noticed sets of cables sticking out of the ground along the road from the harbour to the Punta, in a rather dangerous looking manner about every fifty yards apart, with one set right outside our house. The set outside our house was a favourite peeing spot for Rupert though I always cringed when he did it as I fully expected him to go up in a blinding flash and a cloud of smoke. On making enquiries we learned from Robi that the plan had been to continue the street lighting from the harbour to the end of the Punta.

'Sometime, never,' said Robi. 'Dey run out of money – our money, Mayor in Selca use money for udder sings.'

'That's disgraceful,' I said. 'Can't we do something?'

'Mr Linoleum, you know, he speak wid Mayor, and he say Punta people hev to pay for lights. Commune hev no money.'

'Disgraceful,' I continued to mutter.

'Why we pay? People in willage no pay for lights.' Said Robi waving his arms about and raising his voice as he did when getting heated.

It looked though that Mr Linoleum was onto the case and was arguing for us all so we would have to wait and see.

'Mr Linoleum, he good man you know, he sort it out.'

It would be nice to have some lighting for walking back from the village after a few drinks late at night. On a moonless night the road to the Punta, about ten a minutes stroll, could be very dark particularly through the wooded area near to the cemetery. Quite spooky on the odd occasion though we always carried a powerful torch. It would also be much better for the tourists who rented apartments at the Punta. But it was very much a question of "watch this space", for the moment.

*

'R U P E R T!!!' exclaimed March for the fourth time one evening.

'That is terrible!' and hauling the neck of her polo neck up over her nose she grabbed a magazine and wafted it over Rupert's tail. My reaction to Rupert's farts was to puff very strongly on my pipe in the hope that the effect would be nullified. This was a particularly bad fart though and even Rupert, after noting our exclamations, took a furtive sniff in the direction of his rear end and shot off into the kitchen. We had noticed ever since we had lived in Dalmatia that Rupert's farts had become really smelly. This we put down to the tinned dog-food as it had not been noticeable in Jersey. He did fart in Jersey, so he didn't seem to have anything against Dalmatia, but they were not so smelly. The dog-food was in large tins with usually only a chicken variety on sale. He did eat our meat also but we tended to eat spicy food so that was not going to help. He had also taken a fancy to fish, and in particular sardines, which was no doubt contributing to the problem.

The worst time for him though was during the night. We always seemed to wake up when he had farted in the middle of the night. Perhaps our subconscious, having received signals from our noses that there was a deadly smell around, brought us round to investigate. The immediate action was to pull up the sheets over our heads and complain bitterly to one another with the usual exclamation of 'RUPERT!!' But Rupert was usually fast asleep on the end of the bed blissfully ignorant of his anal activities whilst chasing cats in his doggy dreams. Rupert would certainly have won the farting competitions I had indulged in whilst a small nasty boy at school, if he had qualified for entry.

We had tried dog biscuits but he had never been a great fan of them and never ate vegetables.

We were not worried that he had something wrong with him as he remained his usual perky and active self, but he was getting old so perhaps the combination of different dog food and the ageing process was the reason. Anyway it looked as though we were going to have to grin and bear it whilst in Dalmatia. Now that the nights were getting much warmer though we could sit with the French windows open and have our bedroom window open during the night.

*

May drew to a close with us fitting in another two English sessions for the kids who had now grown to eight, with four boys and four girls. Their enthusiasm hadn't waned and we had great fun, which we wanted to achieve whilst improving their English. One little girl who had joined called Renata had taken to arriving early. She had been fighting to speak English and do the reading aloud but she had done very little at school unlike the others. She said everything as though she was speaking Croatian with a strong accent so it didn't sound English at all. March's heart went out to her as she was intense and keen to learn. March patiently taught her word for word in extra tuition before and after the sessions.

*

It was now June and we had to drag ourselves away to France for a while to do some needed house improvements there. We had also been quite successful in getting some Summer lets for our house in Dalmatia. We had bookings from people in Jersey and some from England so we were well pleased. Erika and Robi were also letting their house as they no longer ran the restaurant and had converted part of the restaurant and bar into a little apartment for the summer. Erika was also confident that she could fill in the gaps in our bookings in August as the place would be inundated with Italians. She would be holding our keys and would be taking the money and doing the changeovers. We had to insist that we gave her a commission for this.

So it was time to drag ourselves away. The children had been told that we would resume classes in early September on our return and the old man in his caravan next door had agreed to water our garden with our outdoor hose. Our personal belongings locked in the garage, and the house ready for let, we said our goodbyes.

Erika was quite tearful and so was March. 'Take good care one of each other,' she said as she gave us both big hugs.

'Bye Wupy,' she said as she gave Rupert a cuddle.

'Why you go France, is much better here,' said Robi as he gripped our hands in a firm handshake.

We were beginning to wonder why we were going but we had already been over the ground in numerous discussions. We had decided that July and August were far too hot for us and it was a good opportunity to make some money from tourists who were not the wilting in the sun types.

It was quite warm enough for us in the Spring and early summer there and September through to November could be pretty warm too, but bearable. So we tore ourselves away and drove down along the quayside to say other farewells to our friends. Suzy, Simon and all Suzy's family came out to wish us fond farewells. Tonko also broke away from his morning card game to say goodbye and other friends and acquaintances waved from the cafes. It took us almost half an hour to break away to get to the ferry at Supetar, where we also had to visit the electricity company to pay our bill.

On arrival at their headquarters just before eleven we noticed that the metal gates were closed including the passenger gate at the little porter's lodge. The porter was standing by the gate and said as we approached: 'Everyone having breakfast, come back half hour.'

It took all our self-control not to burst out laughing.

We certainly had that déjà vu feeling! We had time to spare so we relaxed over a beer in a harbour café and speculated what the reaction would be in England or Jersey if the same thing had happened. We were getting used to businesses, shops and banks closing for lunch but this was the first establishment, which we had encountered that was closed down for a morning break.

After the ferry crossing, where we always relished the view from the upper deck of the islands, and coming into port, the view of the ancient seafront and city of Split, we took the coast road north to Rijeka. This was a new route for us. It would take us to Trieste and up into Austria bound for France. The drive along the coast gave us an excellent view of the plethora of islands all along the coast and stretching way out into the Adriatic (there are 1,185 islands in Croatia but only just over 60 inhabited). We were soon passing the ancient Venetian port of Trogir and the smart and picturesque resort of Sibenik but the going was slow; not a lot of traffic but the road was like a snake, winding in and out of every inlet.

We continued for another hour or so and were still playing snakes and ladders with the road, which became even more winding with a bad surface to add to our slow progress and always seemed to pull the car the wrong way. The traffic was less but the going was painful.

'We'll be lucky if we get to Rijeka before it gets dark at this rate,' I muttered.

We also noticed that all forms of life and habitation had disappeared. There were only a few villages which seemed to be deserted and for the next two or three hours there were no petrol stations, cafes or phone booths. The only people we saw were the occasional shepherd; we assumed they were shepherds but they looked more like bandits to us.

'Put on the central locking!' March pleaded after passing one unsavoury looking character standing at the side of the road, eyeing us up as we crawled by. He had a large stick, which was no doubt for prodding sheep or goats, but he looked pretty menacing with it.

'What on earth do we do if we break down!' exclaimed March.

'We are miles from anywhere!'

'Don't worry darling we are ok.' I said in my most reassuring military voice.

As we rose to the crest of a hill the scenery then suddenly changed from the green of the olive trees, small scrub and cypress trees to what looked like a lunar landscape. There was not a tree in sight nor any signs of habitation as far as the eye could see along the coast and a long way inland. The mountains on the mainland and the islands along the coast were almost devoid of any vegetation at all. Everything was the grey of the limestone rocks and cliffs, with the only other colour being the blue of the sea and sky. The Islands here are called the Kornati and there are 147 of them; quite a striking sight. George Bernard Shaw was prompted to write of them: "On the last day of creation God wanted to crown His work and thus created the Kornati out of tears, stars and breath".

After almost two hours of this we gradually returned

to vegetation. Whilst the "lunar " landscape of the coast and the Kornati had been quite an experience we were glad to be amongst greenery again. Some villages with people around appeared and we had a glorious view across to the large islands of Cres, Losinj and Krk with lots of little ones scattered around them like frigates around a battleship.

We were soon on the outskirts of the large commercial city of Rijeka with its extensive harbour and docks. The drive from Split had taken almost seven hours so I was overjoyed to see a smart roadside café where we refreshed ourselves with a couple of chilled Karlovac beers.

After driving round and round the inner city ring road of Rijeka about three times we eventually spotted the sign for Trieste (we had been confused because the Croatians call it Trst!). It was about an hour and a half to Trieste through a short bit of green and undulating countryside of Slovenia. We were now making good time but it was getting dark so we opted for finding a hotel in Trieste. Alas every one we stopped at was full!! We pressed on to Udine, the next large town, and after paying the toll on the autostrada in three different currencies to a charming young Italian official, we found a small hotel with a comfortable room, and better still a pizzaria restaurant which was still open. Gorging ourselves on pizzas, which were even bigger than Erika's and downing a bottle of Chianti, we both agreed that we didn't want to use that route again.

With one further overnight stop we were at our house

in France and set about our planned improvements. Povlja was always in our thoughts and we were constantly wondering how things were there, but now that Robi and Erika had a computer we were kept in the picture with chatty emails always entitled "weather report", twice a week. Our first one from Erika was about the problems they were having with customers for their little manufacturing business and some progress on the lamps for the Punta:

"Sory im late vith mail, we are little busy vith menus, You know everyone vonts them same day vhen they make order but they vould like to pay next year. Alveys the same problem. Robi is so nervos because the account is alveys empty, and we are vorking vhole day , but that happends every year this time, so probably we will suriwe as always. WE have few days of rain, so you don't need to worry about garden. Nothing specialy is not hepend, I need to go on coffy in willage to hear some gossip news, so then my mail will be more interesting. People come by Ljeka so she is in good mood for moment, they probably stay for manth, Austrians daughter is clean the land and already start to build septic tank, Simon is paint the metal things on riva which is used for ropes for ships. We need to giwe 300 kuna(ewery house) for light on Punta, and ewveryone are arguing and fighting because noone in willage didn't pay for lights except us on Punta(same happends with asfalt), and Mayor ask for some mony. He say that mony is missing for three candels, and ewveryone say that if he don't put that money in his pocket be some of oure lights. It is diskasting but if we don't give that mony we newer get light so You could imagine what is talking around. Robi say that he will for you because we owe you some, so then we are quit. Im

kidding, just hope he sum up good all together. For now that's it, I need to run soil mashine, hope you like attach, poor dog!!!! Love You E&R!!!

So we were going to have to pay for our streetlights at the Punta just as they all had to pay for the asphalt the year before we arrived. But we heard from Erika that Mr Linoleum who was collecting the money was holding half of it back until the work was completed as everyone was sure that Drago, the Regional Mayor, would use the money for some other pet project of his.

We were having good weather in France at the end of June but obviously not as hot as Povlja, according to Erika:

If you are here today you probably will be ded, it is 34 ore 35, just like in hell. This morning we cleaned the beach: turistic community, people from hotel, us, Ljerka, mr Linoleum …..we make fire for wooden things and wires and other garbage put in rubbish bin, cut the trees near bin and make nice shade for sitting, and now looks really nice…But now we are so tired, it is really hot and whole morning from 7 til 12 on the sun, You cant imagine, Robi after lunch lay down on the kauch and who knows when he will woke up. Everyone send you regards, be careful wit the sun and this hot weather, don't stay to long in the kitchen mr Mike, take care one of each other, til soon, Love E&R,..

We pootled around on our house in France throughout August in quite hot weather but not it seemed as hot as in Povlja judging by one of Erika's weather reports:

Hy neighbours, it is ameising hot, and how you write me I can see that you also hawe hell ewen. It is really nice temperature tooday though, we hawe about 35 and sea is like urin!!! We will vrite the bill like you told us and take it day before they leave(Czech tourists in our house). I hawe the name cause you send me before, so probably there will not be any problems, they seem a little bit not communicative, so running away past quickly through my hed somewhere deep inside, you know what I mean......We newer soo them, they go in the willage, they are on terase or on the beach, we think they bring even bread with and lots of cans (because freezer is not in house...) Well we all know what the Chehs are like...The Povlja are a little bit crowdy than usually, but nothing specialy, most of the people in tuist buisnes are crying how bed it is this year. When I wrote that we howe a litar of rain I mean in whole of Dalmacia, the soil are incedible dry, and olive groves are look terrible, little olives are already black and they will fall down before picking because there is no rain and now is too late if rain will fall, the heat cut them on dead, and the wegetables also, but instead of ewerything every day I pick 2 ore 3 tomatos, vell done, vell done ....That's all for now. Take good care one of each other, love E&R (Erica was mimicking March here as one of her favourite comments is "well done, well done!!")

The Czechs who rented our house from the internet were true to form it seems as they brought most of their food and drinks with them. They had not been happy that we only had a small freezer compartment so that must have curbed them a bit. The Croatians had become very unhappy with the Czechs because they were not buying locally and rarely ate out in the restaurants or drank in the bars. The Dutch tourists were also of the same ilk.

Erika's comment on the potentially poor crop of olives must have been worrying for the villagers all of whom had olive groves and depended on them producing their cooking oil. We had promised Erika and her Mother and Father who had several olive groves that this year we would help all the family with the picking, but it sounded as though it would not be quite the jolly time that we had been told it always was. However, knowing the Dalmatians they let very little get them down.

We set off back for Croatia and the chance to help with the olive picking in early September. Taking our preferred direct route through the Frejus tunnel and onward through Italy to the Port of Ancona where we got the overnight ferry, we were soon again driving across our Island impatient to see that wonderful view of Povlja down that steep winding road through the olive groves. We were back again for another three months full of joy at being there.

Chapter 14

Concrete and Pyjamas

Driving along the quay we noticed that Iveca had opened up a rival grocers shop. We had heard that he was going to do this but it took us by surprise, so in we went to get some supplies. Smaller than the other one but it was well designed, smart and well stocked. Iveca, who had been Erika's Best Man at her wedding was grinning like a Cheshire cat sitting at the till.

'You like?' he enquired.

'This is really good.' Said March. 'Well done, well done!'

'If anything you specially need, I will get if I can,' said Iveca.

'Well there is actually,' said March ominously.

'You don't have any of that blueberry juice that the other shop has. We love it, its really good for you and we don't have it in England.'

'No problem, I get.'

Further along the quay another small café/restaurant

had opened. Work had started before we left but was now completed with tables and parasols outside and most of the tables filled with locals. Mario, who had worked as a waiter for Robi and Erika, was the son of the owner and came out of the café to our car where in his cheerful and friendly way welcomed us back.

'This is good ', I said. 'We will come in for a drink later. Have you been busy?'

Mario threw his arms in the air. 'Werry busy for two months. Many Italians all wanting fish, we never stop!'

How they managed was hard to believe, as the café inside was very small, hardly room to swing a cat let alone cook meals in a small kitchenette. But it was another facility and along with Iveca's shop, Povlja was sprouting new business.

It wasn't long before we were at our house again after driving past the new shiny street lamps which now stretched from the harbour every 30 yards to……..only the Austrian house; two houses before ours! No doubt we would hear the latest in this saga shortly.

'Hey neighbours! Velcome back,' boomed Robi over the garden wall as we parked the car.

Erika rushed down and hugged us both. 'Ah little Wupy too,' as she gave Rupert a loving ruffle of his hair. Rupert loved Erika and gave her one of his best fussy greetings.

'You come for lunch in one hour.' Erica commanded.

'My Modder and Fadder and people from Bol, sorry "Bolognese," come too.'

'Lovely,' we both exclaimed with pleasure, as lunch

with Erika's family was always fun and the food excellent.

A long table was set out in the inner part of Robi and Erika's restaurant that was reminding us of the memorable times there last summer. Ada, Erica's sister, her husband Emir and their two little girls were there. March gave the girls a little present from France, bright beads to make necklaces and bracelets, and they shot away with glee to experiment. We chatted away to their parents and the Grandparents about all the latest news but were soon seated to one of Erika's feasts.

'We notice that some of the street lamps have been fixed,' I said to open the conversation round the lunch table as Erica served everybody soup from a large tureen.

Robi laughed.

'Mayor, you know, he spend money on statue of Tudjman in Selca!'

'Unbelievable!' I exclaimed.

'Mr Linoleum, you know, he good man and still has some of our money for lamps, but told Mayor he don't get till all lamps finished. We wait!'

After the delicious soup we had grilled lamb and chicken pieces roasted with garlic. This was accompanied by a boiled potato and spinach dish plus various salads, including Erika's finely sliced spring onion in salt and olive oil.

We also had some runner beans which prompted Erika to say: 'These are from the seeds you gave us. My Fadder grow them in his garden and they grow enormous, almost half metre!' All willage go to see them. We have never seen beans so long.'

We were really pleased. It just showed what good soil, sun and watering could do. They also had great success with some of the other seeds we gave them except for the parsnips. They had never seen parsnips before but the seeds sprouted not into single parsnips but ones with many legs, which amused them all somewhat.

The subject of olives came up. Erika's father explained that because they had eventually had some rain just before we arrived the crop would be saved. They would not be picking just yet as they hoped for more rain, so it looked as though picking would be later than usual in early October. We readily volunteered to help when the time came.

After such a filling welcome lunch washed down with the usual "black wine" we were ready for a siesta. We put our reclining seats under our only olive tree which we noticed was full of good sized olives, no doubt due to the old man's watering and settled into our familiar routine of reading in the shade until we nodded off. We were back in Dalmatia but we didn't feel that we had been away.

After such a feast at lunchtime we decided to venture into the willage to say hello to some of our other friends and to have a drink in Mario's father's bar or "kornoba" as they call a bar. On the walk in we inspected the street lamps, which were causing such a controversy. We noted that if they had spaced them a little further apart, but still giving good coverage, we would have had lamps to the end of the Punta, however the ongoing saga was giving some good entertainment. We also noticed that work had begun on several of the unfinished houses at the Punta; these had been started just before the Balkan war but had stopped when tourism collapsed. So perhaps confidence was returning. Robi's two cousins had such a house finished as four apartments just in time for the recent summer season and had some success in letting.

Mario greeted us at the bar and we settled down at an outside table to watch the activity around the harbour in the early evening sunlight. Large wooden and plastic barrels were already appearing on the quay in front of people's houses. These were to house the olives, once they started picking, which would be covered in seawater to cure them before the went off to the olive pressing factory in Selca to be made into oil. Little fishing boats were also venturing out for a nights fishing and the crew were gathering for the "Povlja" the only large fishing boat which would be out all night and not return with their catch until ten am the next day. Some of them were in the bar snatching a last snorter before their night-time labours.

We were soon joined by Simon and Suzy who we had texed on our mobile to invite them for a drink.

'Let's have your news. How did the scooter and boat hire go?' I asked. (Simon had invested in two scooters and two small boats with outboard engines.)

'We do quite well,' said Suzy.

'We took enough to buy another two scooters next year,' chimed in Simon.

'I have also been made Harbourmaster,' said Simon grinning.

'Nobody else wanted the job so I applied. It took a lot of paperwork and visits to Split but the harbour authorities gave it to me in the end.'

'That's really great. Are you going to do the much needed reorganisation of the moorings so that more visiting yachts can get in?' I enquired.

Simon and Suzy laughed. 'I've already started and its causing quite a bit of a furore amongst the locals who seem to think they own the water directly in front of their houses and don't see why they should move their boats a few metres!!'

'I've got quite a few people behind me but some are muttering: "Why do we have a foreigner as the harbourmaster?" which makes me laugh as none of them were prepared to do the job!' 'I'm also investing my own money into new anchorages and mooring chains – something they wouldn't do either!'

'Well done Simon.' Said March (she was becoming well known for her "well dones" and indeed both Erika and Suzy were already mimicking her).

'But are you making any money at it?'

By chance a visiting yacht was just tying up at the quay and Suzy leaped up with an official looking book and went over to enquire whether they were staying the night, which meant harbour dues for Simon.

'There's your answer,' said Simon. 'We have made quite a bit of money, some of which goes to Split Harbour Authority and some I am giving to the community. The fees are very low compared with the rest of the Adriatic and Med but if I increase the number of moorings and perhaps persuade the commune to build some shower rooms we can attract more yachts. We already have water and electricity on tap for the yachts on the quay and the harbour is a yachtsman's dream haven with all the bars and a couple of restaurants.'

'I agree, they really have to switch on if they want more business here.' I replied.

'The younger element here know what has to be done but the old and bold don't want any change.'

Suzy came back pleased with one nights harbour dues, hardly enough to buy a couple of beers but it all added up for them if Simon was to carve a life in Povlja for them both. His time as a sailing instructor would not go on forever as the army could pull out at any time.

It was then that we noticed that the Dutch couple outside their restaurant were loading their space wagon with bits of furniture and cases.

'What's going on there?' said March.

'You don't know?' said Suzy.

'A bit of gossip we obviously haven't heard yet?' enquired March craning her neck to see more of what was going on.

'Dey leaving,' continued Suzy. 'Dey fall out with partner who was unhappy that dey were not making enough money after spending so much of his money on the restaurant.'

'They have also upset a lot of the locals,' said Simon. 'The partner has put a local chap in to run it as a bar during the winter and he hopes to open it as a restaurant again next year if he can get someone to run it.'

We all decided to walk round to the other side of the harbour to continue our pub-crawl. As we passed the new post office we noticed that it had at last been occupied. 'Ah, the new post office is open. I hope they haven't noticed the faint stain of red wine from my exhibition.' I joked.

'What's happening to the old post office on the quay? That would make a good shower place for the visiting yachts.'

'That's what I thought.' Said Simon. 'But the post office have stipulated that it can only be used as a butchers shop!!'

'What!!' exclaimed March and I in unison.

'Yes, they want to encourage the use of it as a butchers because we don't have one, but nobody is interested. In the meantime it is lying idle. The rent is only ten kunas a year, about 80P,' laughed Simon.

'You should become a butcher at that rate,' said March, always happy to encourage business opportunities.

'Funnily enough I am considering it,' said Simon. 'But I don't know much about being a butcher!'

'You could always get in pre cut and packed meat and sell some fresh and some frozen,' said March enthusiastically.

'That's a good idea I will look into that.'

We took a table at Mr Doc's bar and enjoyed a few beers in the fading light whilst speculating for a while on whether Simon should become a butcher. We also learned that a small bar, which the Dutch had run on the quayside last year, had been rented that summer by an Albanian couple who also sold the most excellent ice cream, which the Albanians were apparently renowned for.

'Do you want any concrete?' said Simon changing the subject. 'There is a beton kamion (concrete mixer lorry) which comes regularly to deliver to the house next to us. I am taking some for the moorings but there could be a meter or so spare if you had a use for it.'

Immediately both March and I said yes. We had already discussed a little project of clearing the overgrown area below our terrace and turning it into another patio area with surrounding flowerbeds.

'We will need a few days to clear the ground and I will work out how much concrete we will need, but a metre sounds about right. I will let you know.' I said to Simon.

'Will the mixer chute reach over our four foot high wall?' I asked him. 'Should do but we can always borrow some wheelbarrows.'

We all strolled back around the harbour in the warm glow of the harbour lamps. People were still sitting at the outside tables in the warm evening air and little fishing boats chugged in and out of the harbour. We said goodnight to Simon and Suzy at their house and went on to the Punta where the new lamps lit our way as far as the Austrian house, leaving us just a short walk in the dark, speculating on how long it would be before we had the rest of them installed.

'We should have a party for the Punta people when they are up,' laughed March.

Next morning we were up early to start our new patio project. The sun was already bright but not too hot yet for our labours but by midday it would be too hot to work. I borrowed a wheelbarrow from Robi and some garden tools.

'Vot you do?' he enquired with that wide toothy grin of his fully expecting to hear of another "English" venture. He wasn't disappointed when I told him about the patio. 'Ah you English, never stop.

Vy you not just hev holiday!!' he said shaking his head and walking off to his garage.

We hacked and dug with picks and forks clearing the massive growth of succulent plants, which covered the area with some really tough rooted tall silver-leafed plants. By lunchtime we had only cleared a third of the area as a lot of the time we had to wheelbarrow or drag the debris to the rubbish bins on some waste ground about a hundred yards away. It was good exercise but we were pretty knackered. Cold beers were definitely needed.

Sitting on our terrace it wasn't long before Erika came to see what we were up to and to sip a glass of wine with us whilst she smoked a couple of cigarettes.

'Vot you do?' she enquired.

We described our plans and showed her our work so far.

'I give you plants for the garden. Ve hev plenty.' Erika's garden was full of a lovely plant with its lovely big pointed leaves and orange flowers. They grew quite tall and spread like weeds, and would be ideal for the border around our new patio.

'You do English lessons again for kids?' she enquired.

'Yes' said March, 'Suzy is putting up the notices today so we hope to have them all back next Saturday. And, we have some new books for them to read.'

March went to get the bags full of children's storybooks, which had been given to us by John Sankey, the recently retired Headmaster of De la Salle College in Jersey. We often bumped into him having lunch on our trips to Jersey in La Taverna, the restaurant owned by Bruno an Italian friend of ours. One lunchtime we had joined him, the new headmaster and Bruno at John's table and had been describing our adventures in Croatia including the children's English lessons. They were most impressed and organised a big pile of books for us to take back to Croatia.

Erika was very pleased. 'Dees are much better. Dey are proper English, not American English.

'Vell done, vell done,' she said, teasing March.

It was then that I saw two large yachts, flying the German flag, motoring towards the harbour mouth.

'Quick, give me the mobile phone I have to warn Simon so that he can get the mooring fees!' I called to March, and proceeded to text him. In a couple of minutes Simon texed us: 'Got them! Thanks.' From then onwards this was to be a regular feature when we saw yachts from our terrace and even Erika joined our early warning system for Simon.

It took us three days to clear and level the area for the new patio but Simon did not have a delivery date for the next load of concrete so we busied ourselves building a low stone wall around the edge of the proposed patio. This would be a retaining wall for the flower borders but would also contain the concrete rather than using timber shuttering. This was back breaking work collecting the correct size stones from the beach and wheel-barrowing them into our garden. It took two days to gather enough stones to build a wall only about a foot high, of the two foot I had planned. Our meagre attempts made me realise what a mammoth effort it was to build all those dry stone walls in the Yorkshire Dales.

It was whilst we were at this stage that Simon arrived one morning on a scooter. 'The beton is coming this afternoon. I will bring him to you and give a hand.'

We prepared ourselves for the arrival but as the afternoon drew on we began to wonder if the beton was coming. We had a text from Simon saying that five pm was the time he had been given but five came and went and so did six and seven. Then we had another text from Simon at about seven thirty to say that it had arrived and was offloading the main load in the village.

Eventually the beton arrived at ten past eight and dusk was coming fast. Simon arrived with a rake and Robi also came to help with Erika who helped March to supervise us from our terrace. Joshko, a builder friend of theirs was having a beer with them at the time and he also pitched in to help as the concrete was being poured down the chute into the front garden. It was rapidly getting dark and difficult to see so we all bent our backs to the task of shovelling and spreading the concrete. We got it all over the wall and roughly spread but it was too dark to smooth it properly in site of the torches March and Erica were directing from the terrace above. Then Simon called to Suzy to get on her scooter to get some halogen lamps from his workshop. She was soon back and once they were rigged up we had enough light for Joshko, very professionally, to smooth the concrete to a level finish with a piece of wood.

How we thought we were going to be able to do this ourselves in the dark did not bear contemplation. If it hadn't been for these delightful friends who turned up unasked, and worked so hard and cheerfully, the concrete would have been a lumpy mess by morning.

Having paid the man with the beton truck, it was time to break out the beers and wine. We all sat down around our terrace with a sense of achievement but laughing at the laying of the concrete in the dark.

*

The first Saturday was soon upon us, and the children, eight of them again, were with us as keen as ever for their English lessons. They loved the books. For an hour or so we both took them for reading out loud and making sure they understood the words and did correct pronunciation. We ended this time with us all sitting on our terrace and getting them to name things in English which we pointed out to them: the sea, sky, yachts and so on. It was all great fun with lots of laughter.

We were sure that they had learned a lot of new words and how to pronounce them; though we were still getting the "v" and "w" problem but they were getting it right more often than not. We were aware that we were not professional teachers but we were sure that the reading and contact with English people would help them, particularly as they were so well motivated and were having fun learning. We had five children and ten grandchildren between us so we were not totally lacking in what was required. We resolved to send a postcard to John Sankey in Jersey thanking him on behalf of the children for the books. We knew he would be pleased that they had been well received.

*

The following week we had to go to Selca to the bank and to get some veg from the new smart stone open market there. There were never more than about three traders in the market but they had a selection of what was in season and the quality was good. Next to the market was a new small park with neatly cut grass and new shrubbery. But centrepiece, were three bronze busts, the biggest of which was of the late President Tudjman! So perhaps this was where our money for the Punta street lamps had been squandered!!

Visits to the butcher in Selca were now not quite the farmyard, which March had created that first time with her animal impressions, but the young butcher always grinned impishly at March. I was sure he was muttering to himself: 'not that mad English woman again'. But we had learned a lot of new words so we usually got by.

We had to visit the little ironmonger shop for some bags of cement and were greeted by our little friend the proprietor like long lost relatives.

'You back. Sehr gut, dobro.' As he launched into speaking to us in his usual three languages hoping that some of it would rub off. As usual the other things we required, some window catches, were not amongst his limited stock.

'I get, drei tag, OK?'

Three days was certainly OK. We were never in any great hurry to do anything in Dalmatia.

It was a sunny morning and the tables were out under the trees at the café in the square so we did a little people watching over a couple of beers. The priest, a short middle-aged handsome chap, was mowing the grass outside the church at the other end of the square and some nuns were sweeping the church steps. There were a few of the locals standing around chatting and a noisy game of cards was going on at another table, but no sign of any tourists. By mid September the tourist season is all but over on the island though on the mainland along the Dalmatian coast and in Dubrovnik it would still be pretty busy.

As we drove back to Povlja through the olive groves there was some activity and little tractors and trailers, looking more like lawnmowers with two wheels, long devils angel's handlebars and a trailer attached. They chugged in and out of the olive groves getting ready for the picking. They moved a little less than walking speed so it must take ages to get to and from the willage. At the gates of some of the groves battered little cars were also parked, many of them without number plates, which was an offence as Robi had found out last year, but then the police hardly ever came to Povlja.

We then came across the familiar sight of a little old man leading his old donkey, which was piled high with branches pruned from his olive trees, and sitting right on the top of the pile was his old black dog.

As we offloaded our shopping a young woman came in through our gate with a large holdall. We smiled and shook hands as she emptied the contents of the holdall onto our table on the terrace. There were packets of ladies pyjamas in all sorts of colours and sizes.
'You like, werry cheap, good quality,' she announced enthusiastically.
March sorted through the selection.
'These look nice, they are good quality and they feel warm too,' as she thought of the next winter. She selected a pink set and we paid a very reasonable price.
'Where are you from?' enquired March.
'Ve come from Zagreb, sell down coast.'
We shook hands and wished her well as she went up to Robi and Erika's.
After she had left we heard lots of laughter coming from their workshop and Erica came to the garden wall.
'You buy?' she grinned.
'Yes, lovely warm pyjamas.' March said as she held them aloft.
'Ven she ask us if ve buy pyjamas, Robi say: no pyjamas, ve sleep in nude!! Girl go red and run avay!'

"TAXIS!"

Chapter 15

Olive Picking

It was now almost mid October and on one of our many trips into the willage on an almost daily basis we noticed even more barrels all along the harbour quays and an increased activity of people and little lawnmower tractors chugging backwards and forwards to the olive groves. Some of the barrels were almost full of olives so picking had begun by some people, but no news of any picking date from Erika's father. On our return from Selca one day we saw Tonko's car parked along a little lane through the olive groves near the willage.

'Lets go and see what is going on,' I said, and we swung up the bumpy stone track.

Picking our way along a little footpath we came across Tonko, Dalmina and about a dozen of their friends all busy picking olives. Tonko saw us and came over to us beaming.

'Gruss Gott, wir machen viel arbeit,' said Tonko.

'Mochst du ein schnapps?'

We didn't want to interrupt his work but noticed that one or two of his friends had a glass in their hands and were obviously having a brief schnapps break so we accepted. Tonko took us on a tour of his trees. He was immensely proud of his olive groves and he had several of them. They were by far the best cared for we had seen and his olives looked good, probably due to the automatic watering system he had installed, something which was beyond the pockets of most of the other villagers who were at the mercy of the weather as to whether they had a good crop or a disastrous one.

He told us that it took him and his seventeen helpers almost two weeks to pick his crop. Most of the villagers had much smaller plots, which could usually be handled by family and friends in a couple of weekends. He and his friends would all move on to the next friend's groves to continue picking in a sort of little cooperative.

We didn't want to keep him from his work so bade them all farewell.

'Do videnja !!' they all called out from the trees.

'Do vidjena,' we replied, and then left them to their toils in the hot sun. But we knew we had this to come when we helped Erika's father.

'We are going to need our straw hats and lots of water when we do the picking,' said March.

'Yes, you're right,' I agreed but secretly hoped that there might also be a sip of wine and schnapps occasionally to keep us going.

*

Back home we asked Erika when her father would start picking.

'He vait till best time, probably next few days.'

'Our young olive tree is looking good, come and see, there are lots of olives,' I said with pride. But of course the old Bosnian man next door had watered it during the summer when he was there. About half of the olives were black.

'I love black olives, how do we prepare them for eating and bottling,' I asked her.

'I never hev done it. I ask for you,' she replied.

Erika obviously phoned her Mother as she was soon back at our house with details of how they prepared them for eating and for bottling.

'You put olives in boiling vater for two minutes, then put on tray with salt and put outside in de sun. Couple of days outside and ready for eating and bottling in ordinary oil, not olive oil.'

'Right,' I said lets get cracking. We all picked some black olives from our tree and I blanched them in a pan of boiling water whilst Erika and March poured some wine out on our terrace. I was soon out there with a tray of the olives, which I put on the terrace wall.

'There we go - I can't wait for them to be ready!' I said taking my glass of wine.

'Here's to our first crop from our very own olive tree.'

'Vate and see in couple of days,' said Erika cautiously. 'Den ve see if OK to eat!'

That evening Suzy and Simon popped around on their walk with their Irish Setter.

'What's all this,' said Simon peering at out tray of olives.

We explained what we were doing and asked Suzy if she knew how to prepare them.

'No, I never have done that, my Grandmother vill know. I ask her.'

I was interested to note that two young local women in their thirties had not had the secret of preparing olives for eating passed on to them by their parents.

Next morning Suzy was around on her scooter bright and early with her grandmother's recipe. This was different. The olives were put on a tray and put into an oven at a temperature of about 50 degrees centigrade for about thirty minutes and then sprinkled with salt and put out on the wall for a few days. We picked more of the black olives and followed Suzy's instructions.

'We will have an olive tasting in a couple of days.' I said confidently.

'My grandmother has some ready to eat. You must call in today.'

So later that morning we walked into the willage to sample the olives.

Franika, Suzy's grandmother, was chatting on the quay in front of her house. 'Dobar dan,' she beamed and rushed away up the steep stone steps to her house, a most impressive feat for an eighty-year old woman. She returned in a trice equally sprightly with a dish of black olives, and muttering something in Croatian, we were encouraged to sample the olives. They were tender and quite tasty but still a little bitter, which perhaps more time on the tray would no doubt cure. Conversations with Franika were limited when she didn't have Suzy with her as she spoke only Croatian. So it really consisted of a lot of sign language and "dobros".

Olive sampling over we retired to have a coffee in Mario's father's café. There we saw Tonko indulging in a game of cards with his chums, but he broke away and came over to join us. We told him about our activities with the olives and he immediately launched into how it should be done.

Again it was a different recipe. What we had to do was to bake the olives on a tray in the oven for an hour at 100 degrees centigrade and then cool and put on the wall outside; at least that bit was common to the three options. When we did this however the olives became overcooked so perhaps my German translation got the temperature or the length of cooking time wrong, or both.

A couple of days later Erika came down for a pre dinner glass of wine and a chat. She felt the olives and nibbled a couple.

'They are OK,' she ruled, so we also had a taste. They had certainly softened and were a little bitter but quite edible. It was then that Erika's mobile phone rang (everyone in Croatia seemed to have one now as they were incredibly cheap to buy and calls on a pay-card system also very cheap). It was Erika's mother who told her that they would be olive picking on Saturday.

'You come too?' enquired Erika'

'Of course,' said March. 'We wouldn't miss that for anything – oh, but what about the children's English lessons!'

'No vorry,' said Erika. 'I phone families and cancel.

But dey vill all be picking dis veekend, children as vell.'

'Picking is great day, ve hev lunch, my fadder do grill and ve all hev good time.'

'Shall we bring some food and wine?' I asked.

'Just vine!!' Erika laughed.

Erica drew a little sketch map of how to get to their olive groves.

'Ve just near Saint Anzony chapel off first bend you see willage.'

*

So Saturday came and we were up early collecting hats, sunglasses, wine and suntan lotion. We decided to leave Rupert in the house as the Bolognese had a big male Dalmatian which would almost certainly not like our stroppy Westie and vice versa.

When we got to the top bend described by Erika we pulled in but could not see the chapel. There was a track so I volunteered to do a recce.

Going down the track, which bore no resemblance to Erika's map, I eventually came to a little shrine, which I took to be St Anthony's chapel, so in good military fashion I stopped to listen and peer into the olive groves either side. I couldn't see anyone but the sound of voices seemed to be coming from every olive grove. Then I heard that loud voice of Robi's, spurting out Croatian like a machine gun.

Walking towards the sound I eventually heard other voices of their family and Erika's laugh, and then I saw them, and they me.

'Hi neighbour, ver Miss March?' boomed Robi.
'In the car whilst I found you.' I replied.
'Leave car on road and climb over vall here.'

The walls were pretty solid affairs. They were dry stone in construction and white limestone, reminding me of the Yorkshire Dales, and were about four foot high and two to three feet thick. They surrounded every olive grove and were made from the stones, which had been cleared from the ground so that they could plant the trees. Apart from defining everyone's plots they must have given a lot of protection from the Buras. Any stones left over, and there were tons of them, had been built into very neat stone mounds rather like burial mounds. On some plots they had constructed small round houses rather like a stone igloo with just one opening. In one of these, not far from our house, Franika had fled from the Italians during the occupation in WW2 and had given birth to her first child.

Having got March and negotiated the wall we said hello to them all. There was Erika's mother and father, Robi's mother from Split, the Bolognese including the two girls who were racing in and out of the trees with the huge Dalmatian, and Erika's other sister Josipa from Split. We were given aprons with large front pouches for putting the olives as we picked and a glass of home made schnapps no doubt to get us in the mood.

We all worked on one tree or two at the most. The vast majority of olives were easily reachable because of the way the trees had been pruned over the years so only Robi had to go up a ladder to get to the few, which were out of reach. Erika's job was to pick up all the windfalls. When our pouches were full we dumped the olives into large plastic bags.

We chatted about all sorts of things with Robi and Emir always adding a touch of humour, particularly Emir who was full of jokes.

Everyone spoke in English mostly for our benefit so Erika had to translate all the time for her parents.

At about midday Erica's father broke off to light from a fire from the old branches and twigs which the girls had collected. It wasn't long before we could smell chicken and lamb roasting on the fire, making our mouths' water. Erika came around with more schnapps and red wine before we were eventually all called to a picnic laid out under a tree.

It was truly a feast. Apart from the meat roasted on the fire, there were numerous salads, boiled potatoes and bowls of bread. The sun was now pretty hot but the olive tree gave good shade - a perfect setting for a picnic with such lovely people. Having devoured all the food and emptied all the wine bottles we had just a short rest before the picking restarted in earnest.

Erika's father had about twenty large trees in this particular grove, which he had only recently inherited from a relative. I noted that they were old big trees and that there were some gaps where Erika's father had already planted new young trees. It took us all till four pm to pick all the olives; about six hours picking all told. My arms were certainly feeling the strain so I for one was glad to stop. I think everyone else was too.

They brought up Robi's battered old Citroen and

Emir's Fiat to load all the bags and some of the family. The olives were then taken down to the harbour and emptied into a large barrel, which was topped up with seawater. We took the rest down to the village where some of us gathered round a couple of tables at Mario's father's café to enjoy a well-earned beer in the late afternoon sun and to chat about the day's picking.

The following day, Sunday, was a repeat performance but in their old olive grove up a rough track behind the village church. Again we tramped along the track listening to the voices of the villagers picking olives either side until we recognised familiar voices, particularly Robi and Emir who seemed to be joking about something in their loud voices.

This grove had about fifteen trees, again old and big and well laden with olives. It took a while for our arms to loosen up after they had gone stiff from the labours the previous day but they all seemed to be suffering too. It was another great day with another barbecue of roast meats prepared by Erika's father, salads, potatoes and black wine, which we had contributed. Being a smaller olive grove we were finished by three pm. It was a warm sunny day so we took the opportunity to jump in the sea for a relaxing swim.

We were showering ourselves in our garden shower when Robi and Erika returned home after delivering the olives to the barrel on the harbour.

'How many did we pick this weekend?' I enquired.

'About 460 kilos,' said Erika looking pleased.

'How much oil is that?'

'About 90 liters, which is usually 20%, if ve lucky. Robi say that my mother pray good, so good so if she continue like that, next year ve vill not have space for keeping oil!'

'You can have the olives from our little tree. We will pick them tomorrow.' I said proudly. And so we did and got 10 kilos, which represented another couple of bottles of olive oil.

Next door to us, the open plot of land where the old Bosnian man spent the summers in his caravan had been transformed in the spring to a partially built single story house of about the same square footage as our house. Work had stopped for the summer months as all building work must in tourist areas. It had been the old man's dream to build a house there and he had amassed a sizeable amount of building bricks and Brac stone facings neatly stacked next to his caravan. But his dream had been shattered a few years before our arrival when his wife had collapsed and died suddenly whilst they were bathing in the sea. His daughter and her husband, who we had met a few times on their trips to the island from Bosnia, were now realising his plans. They had told us that they would build the house as and when money was available but they hoped to complete it in a couple of years. We were more than happy with that as the plot would look a little more salubrious with a house replacing the pile of bricks and caravan. The house would also provide a bit of a buffer to the Buras, which swept through there and wind-burnt all our plants. The building so far had been constructed by a small team of builders who had come across from Bosnia. They had laid the concrete foundations and constructed concrete pillars which had been bricked up, except for the window and door openings. The house was then capped with a concrete slab onto which the roof would be constructed.

One morning shortly after the olive picking we were awakened about seven am to the sound of one of those noisy little lawnmower tractors with trailer attached and the sound of timber being offloaded. I quickly dressed and went round to have a look. There was a large chap with ginger receding hair and a huge walrus moustache offloading building materials in the three-metre gap between our house and the new house.

He was big and bluff looking rather like the sergeant major in the book: "The Good Soldier Svek."

'Dobar dan,' I began hopefully. 'Do you speak English?'

'Dobar dan, Ja, leetle English, also leetle Deutsch.' He replied and held out his hand to shake mine in a vice-like grip. 'My naame ist Boris.'

Oh no, I thought, not another of those mixed English–German conversations.

'My name is Mike, are you working on the house here?' I asked pointing to the half finished house.

'Ja, I doo leetle vork dis vinter.

I left him to his toils and for the next couple of days he pottered about bringing sand, cement bags, a cement mixer and other bits. He then cleared the ground between the two houses and laid a concrete plinth covering the area between the houses. The Croatians love concrete and paved areas so we assumed that it was either a patio or a parking space, until we awoke the next morning to the nerve grating sound of a masonry drill drilling into our bedroom wall, which was on the boundary of the properties. We immediately got dressed and shot round to next door.

'What are you doing drilling into our wall?' I asked somewhat heatedly.

He was somewhat taken aback. 'I fix rods for pillars of garage,' he replied widening his arms outwards and hunching his shoulders in a gesture of it being quite obvious what he was doing.

'No you are not, we don't know anything about this,' I said getting even more heated.

'Eet is in zer plans,' he said confidently. 'I see plans, garage ist attached to ure house.'

This stumped us for a minute so he continued.

'Anyvay better fur ure house. Varmer fur sie und more protection against Bura.'

'But we don't want a garage attached to our house,' chimed in March obviously very annoyed.

It was then that Frau Moser, from the Austrian house not far away was walking past to go to the bins and asked what was going on. When we explained she launched a tirade at Boris in German telling him that it was not allowed to build within three metres of your next-door neighbour. Boris disagreed and said that as our wall was on the boundary you could build onto it. Frau Moser was not to be put off. She was a stout pugnacious woman and spoke with the authority of someone who had lived here for fourteen years and knew all the building regulations.

But Boris eventually just shrugged and said: 'You speak wit owner. Er hat permission. Speak wit building inspector.'

He then went back to work whilst we continued discussing the matter with Frau Moser who was as indignant as we were.

We then went round to Robi and Erika to tell them about the problem. They were also incensed and Robi said he would telephone Paul, the son in law of the old man, as he was the one organising the building works. Robi also said he would also speak to the building inspector. Don't vorry, ve sort out,' he said confidently.

This made us feel much better and calmed down our anger over the situation.

It took Robi a couple of days to get hold of Paul who said he had not told Boris to drill into our wall. He said he would telephone Boris to tell him to fill in the holes. He did say though that he had the plans, which allowed him to build a garage against our wall.

Robi had also telephoned the building inspector and arranged an appointment for us to see him in a few days time.

The next day I popped my head over the garden wall to see what Boris was up to. He had removed the reinforcing rods, which he had put into our wall and was busy filling in the holes.

'Dobar dan,' I said as cheerfully as possible.

'Dobar dan,' he replied and then started shaking his

head. 'I no understand you Eenglish, garage much better fur ure house. You come here telling us vat to do, is different here in Hrvatska.'

'But we don't want it, anyway we are going to see the building inspector.' And with that I withdrew.

Robi and Erica were too busy with various orders for his folders so Suzy very kindly agreed to come with us to Supetar where the building inspectors hung out. Simon took photographs on his digital camera of the space between the two houses and also of the stone blocks, which had been cemented to our wall as part of the entrance to the proposed garage. So the day came for our appointment at nine am so we had an early start.

The offices were in an old tourist hotel, which had seen much better days. The building looked very neglected, hardly the right place for the local commune administration and the building inspectors. We were twenty minutes early and had to wait on the long balcony which ran the length of the third floor, as someone else had an appointment before us. Eventually we entered what had been a small utility hotel bedroom and was now an office crammed with desks and office furniture with files and papers piled everywhere.

The building inspector was a young cheerful chap who shook us by the hand warmly. This, I felt, was a good start as I had fully expected a grumpy uncooperative state official. He spoke English but Suzy decided to speak in Croatian so that there would be no misunderstanding. They chatted away in Croatian for some time and then he went to get a large plan down from a cupboard.

'Look,' he said in English. 'This is the Punta. Only one person have permission to build and it is not your neighbour!'

We laughed. This was good news for us but also amusing, as it meant that all the other people who were building at the Punta did not have permission. Suzy explained to us that the building inspector had said that the next-door neighbours plans must be very old as all building works had to have new plans from January 1998. His house was now an illegal construction. Also the new law was that you could not build within three metres. He advised us to write to the head building inspector in Split with all the details and photographs.

We shook the building inspector by the hand and thanked him profusely. This required an immediate celebration so we walked down to the harbour in Supetar and settled into one of the many cafes there with a welcoming beer.

When I told Boris after we got back to Povlja he was not amused: 'You foreigners, you come here and tell us vat to do, its different here.'

'That is not what the building inspector said. There is no permission to build and we will tell Paul that too.'

Robi did it for us in a telephone call that night. Paul was very good about it, if a little alarmed, as his fifteen year-old plans were invalid and he would have to submit new ones. He and his family were very nice people and we didn't want to fall out with them so we were pleased that he didn't bear any grudges. The building inspector had said that the plans would probably be approved but not the building onto our wall.

We decided though, particularly as so many people in Croatia were building without proper permission, as belt and braces to write to our lawyers in Makarska to get them to send a letter to Paul setting it all out including the new regulations.

Anyway we had made our point as Boris was no longer working at the house waking us up at an ungodly hour and no longer trying to attach a garage to our east wall.

It wasn't long after that, that someone told us that there had been something on the radio about Bosnians building houses down the Dalmatian coast without any planning permission and that in Makarska the police had blown up one illegal house! The Bosnians had virtually no building regulations in their own country so were able to get away with it but the Croatians were obviously not prepared to let them do it in Croatia.

In Bosnia the houses also remained unfinished for a long time as a tax dodging measure but the Dalmatian houses were always finished off well and there was at least some building control including the style of the houses and materials used.

Chapter 16

Vedran's Letter

October drew to a close in continued warm sunny weather. We continued to swim every day in sea temperatures of 26 degrees centigrade; at least that is what the TV showed us every morning on the CCTV cameras as they covered the various resorts from the Istrian peninsular down to Dubrovnik. This was sheer bliss. Our days were spent swimming, trips to the shops, visits to the cafes and siestas in the afternoon. I did manage to do some painting and March some of her fabric artwork but even that seemed a bit of a chore in this laid-back world.

I had received some commissions from time to time from the officers commanding the soldiers at the hotel; they did 6-month tours and wanted to take back a memento of their tour. What better than an oil painting by me, of a scene around Povlja!

I was busy sketching out a painting one day of a scene overlooking the harbour and was about half way up the hill on one of the many bends in the road when a party of hot and exhausted looking soldiers on mountain-bikes passed by. One of them was an instructor who recognised me.

"It's a bit dodgy this spot. We don't stop here anymore because a lot of the soldiers have seen Black Widow spiders in the olive trees. We call it Black Widow corner!"

"Right", I said trying to maintain some sang froid, but nevertheless packing up my things and moving away from the trees.

"Thanks for the tip-off!"

We had seen some little notices stuck to lamp-posts in Bol and Supetar warning of Black Widows with a little picture of one, but we had never seen one.

I asked Robi if he had seen one.

"Not here you know. Here ok"

I was quite relieved as I don't like spiders at the best of times; snakes, beetles and other creepy crawlies are ok but spiders give me the creeps.

One new feature, which appeared at the Punta one morning, was the sound of a 'Mr Whippy-type' vehicle with its jingle. It parked in front of our house and people appeared or leaned out of their windows. We went down with Erika and Robi to investigate. He had ice-creams and lollipops but also quite a selection of frozen food including fish, calamari, and also some interesting looking vegi-burgers. Robi and Erika bought an ice cream each but we also went for the calamari and vegi-bergers. They tuned out to be delicious so we made a note of which day he was due to call every week.

Our English lessons for the children continued and by the end of October we had twelve children. Erika came down every day before lunch and dinner for a fag and a glass of wine and if she stayed too long we would hear Robi calling from his workshop: 'Ereeka!' No doubt feeling it was time for some food. We didn't want to drag ourselves away from this idyllic life but we had decided to spend the winter in France where we had plenty of work to do on the house.

We packed up and left on 31st October and said our fond farewells to Erika and Robi.

'Bura coming!' said Robi laughing and pointing out to sea. Sure enough there were the white horses on the sea over by the mainland. By the time we got into the car to drive away the wind was already buffeting the car. Summer was obviously over so we suddenly didn't feel too bad at leaving. More fond farewells in the willage and we were on our way across the top of the island in a strengthening wind.

As we descended the long winding road to Supetar we could see how rough the sea was towards Split. We had intended to return by the overnight ferry to Ancona in Italy but doubts were being raised:

'I don't think I want to spend a night on the boat, it looks pretty rough to me.' Said March, who was not a good sailor. If the sea were not flat calm March would spend her time with her head in a paper bag being quite ill.

'OK, we will go back by road,' I said.

'But not along that tortuous coastal road. We will go

across your "bandit country" up the road to Zagreb and go up through Austria.'

March looked immensely relieved though she still had to suffer the ferry crossing to Split. Complete with her wristbands, which are supposed to help you, and chewing ginger chewing-gum (again ginger is supposed to help), which we found in our travel bag, she braved the crossing without being sick. However, she did look a little green as we set off on the road to Zagreb.

"It's a pity the motorway from Zagreb to Split isn't open yet", I said.

"I have heard that it is well advanced".(it was going to be a great improvement when it opened shortly.

By the time we reached the drab town of Knin, dark clouds had gathered and it wasn't long before we driving through torrential rain. Going was slow through the still deserted, derelict villages of "bandit country" but we did notice more cafes and quite a few telephone boxes had sprung up since we last came through. After four hours of the heavy rain we reached the national park of Plitvica where the rain eased and we were able to enjoy the glorious colours of the autumn leaves through the forests.

When we got to Karlovac, a large industrial town, which makes the excellent beer of the same name, we swung northwest up to Ljubljana in Slovenia. One day we would have to stop in this old historic city but as we had taken so long in the rain it was already getting dark.

In an hour we would reach Austria where we would look for a small Gaststatte for the night. We found a lovely little place not far from Villach. It was typically Austrian with pine-panelled walls and that quaint old painted furniture with designs painstakingly decorated on every surface. It had a small restaurant, which also doubled as the village pub with merry Austrians swigging steins of beer and schnapps chasers. After a tiring drive, good solid Austrian food washed down with a couple of steins of beer, we had a good night's sleep in an enormous pine bed snuggled under those enormous down-duvets they have.

As we were staying the next night in the Tyrol we had plenty of time to dawdle we took a yellow road along the Austrian Italian frontier and drove through the area where some very serious fighting had been done between the Austrians and Italians in the First World War; a campaign I had studied in my earlier military career.

After a couple of hours we decided that a coffee break was in order and we found a very old Gastatte high up in the mountains on the Austrian side of the Plockenpass. Inside it looked as though time had stood still. The wood panelling was old and dark, and lovely wrought iron lamps hung low above every table. The wooden floor was scrubbed almost white and was well worn with the feet of generations gone. In the corner there was one of those huge ovens tiled in olive green tiles.

A cheerful bucksome Austrian lady in a dirndel asked us what we wanted. We ordered hot chocolate and enquired whether they had apfelstrudel, a favourite of ours in Austria. We beamed as she said yes and ordered schlagsahne (whipped cream, sometimes known just as 'schlag') to go with the strudels.

Whilst waiting we looked at all the old photographs of the officers and soldiers who had been garrisoned around the area during the First World War. This must have been a favourite place for them when they were not in the front line and it was not difficult to imagine them all with their steins of beer probably doing a bit of knee slapping and singing raucous soldier's songs.

We were not disappointed when our hot chocolates and strudels came. They were quite the best we had ever had. We marked the place on our map as it would be an ideal place to stay on our trips to and from Croatia and no doubt the meals would be good too if what we had sampled was anything to go by. As we left at about eleven thirty there were already Austrians and Germans filling the room and ordering bauernschmaus, schnitzels and enormous sausages with piles of chips or rostkartoffeln. It was tempting to stay with our gastric juices running riot but we had already dallied over an hour so had to get on.

*

In a day and a half we were at our house in France. What had started out as a possible nightmare trip across the Adriatic had turned into a journey to remember. We quickly sent off an email to Robi and Erika to say, as we always did, that we had arrived safely. It was a couple of days before we had a reply; unusual for Erika:

"Sorry not write before, I got youre message but we are in big mess in workshop so when I'm not inside I yust laying on kauch

all day, and this weekend was holiday. All Saints Day so we were occupied with semetery, flowers, cendels and so on... It was such a nice weather and semetery newer was so full of flowers, and newer look nicer if semetery could look nice... Bolognesers were here and Josipa too and we all together was on semetery in the evening around nine oclock, it look amaising with all those cendels, thousands of them without the wind like you are somewhere else....you know what I mean. The weather is very nice during the day its so hot and sunny, but in the ewening you nead one sweter cause is a little bit chily. Robi is puting doors on enterence of ex pizzeria, so he is painting logs cause he didn't do that for two years. As you see we are buissy as always. Whan you are in the mood write me paistry resepy for Joshko... til soon love E&R"

The summer had obviously not ended with the Bura as we left so we could possibly have squeezed a few more days there. Joshko had taken up cooking, unusual for a Croatian man, but he probably took courage from experiencing my cooking. Just before we left we had a whole crowd of them around one evening and Joshko was most impressed, not with anything I had cooked, but with the pastry March had made for a large pie, so we quickly sent off an email with the recipe to oblige.

Towards the end of November the weather had changed again in Povlja according to Erika's email:

"We hawe a ameysing strong Jugo (opposite of Bura wind) for a more than two weeks and all of us feeal sick, nervos and depressed and we are praying for one good Bura. Jugo is so strong

that for three days Hvar and Sumartin ferry didn't vork, and temperatures are about 19 to 25. Sick weather. Everyone sends helou to you, Bolognesers were yesterday so we talking about you during lunch, we hawe barbycue (we assumed they weren't cooking dolls!) so we miss you. News in Povlja are missing this time, cause I don't mowe from Punta for ages. Everybody are talking about olives and oil. Take care one of each other, love E&R.

It was nice to be missed but we were glad to have missed that particularly bad Jugo. During the next two months, whilst having a particularly dull wet and cold winter in France, we were cheered up by Erika's weather reports. They had a warm December but then one of the worst winters in Croatia's history:

"Finally ewerything is back in normal so I'm ready to write again. First we are wery busy, than holidays and than weather problems. After realy hot Dec (we were wearing just one sweter) the whole country hawe weather katastrophies. Inside the country so big snow that some willages are for few days cut off from rest of world, ewen from reporters, and by the see big rain and of course in the end bura strong like tornado. The whole traffic is in kolaps, and all time news are: stay at home if is not nessessery for you to travel. It is so cold by us because bura is blowing about 100 and more pro our. We hawe tunders and ligtnings and of course problems with elektrisity, and one old house in middle of the willage near church was hit by tunder. Yust on radio I am listening that ferries don't travel because of wind….. hope that you and Mike are good and not tired, by the way I also hawe some curtains to do so whan you come…and *maybe I find some tiles to do(we had been making curtains and tiling bathrooms)....no, no when you come we do yust cooking, that is abetther idea!!! Ok I finished now this without good gossip news, so take good care one of each other..love E&R*

Christmas came and went and then we had a surprise letter from Vedran who we hadn't seen since he said he would come for a drink to our house. It read:

"Hey Friends

Sorry, sorry, sorry for my uncoming to Povlja to see you. I hope that you are not angry on me. You don't know who writing to you now, its Vedran. Erica gave me your address because I working for Robi last ten days, just to Christmas. We work all days – from 7 in morning to 2000 hrs, many times we talking about you, so, you are with us. Sorry for my writink (crossed out) writing. Maybe I make fault in my writing, but, you can try to write my language, than you will see. Joke.

OOOOH, last couple of days was too cold. It was temperature under 0'C or maybe about 0'C with strong north wind, but now is OK.

Lemon before your house is fresh, lizard on window also. I hope you will come back to Brac soon to see us. We will buy some fish and wine, if you want, and make some meal.

Vedran"

It was lovely to hear from this likeable rogue and

we couldn't wait to take him up on the offer of getting together for a meal. We loved his joke about the lemon tree and lizard, which I had painted in trompe l'oeil on the outside wall of our house, and which were clearly visible from Robi and Erika's. His letter and the continued regular "weather reports" from Erika reminded us what lovely friendly people they were and how lucky we were to have been given the chance to count them as our close friends. From a disastrous start when we first arrived in Croatia we had found a little paradise.

Chapter 17

Driving Lessons

As time marched on into another year we began to feel really part of the local community though most locals referred to us as "The English". We certainly knew more people, particularly the younger element who were friends of Robi and Erika, however, we recognised more people and vice versa, indicated by the number of dobar dans we receiver in the street.

It was probably going to take 25 years though, as in the Yorkshire Dales where I come from, to be regarded as local; in the Dales you are an "off-cumden" for 25 years before being accepted!

One sunny morning in May, March was tending her garden and I was in the house pottering about when she heard a helicopter pass by (occasionally the army brought in people for R&R by helicopter). A few minutes later she looked up from her work to see a huge soldier in full combat kit, camouflage cream and automatic rifle, leaning over the wall and staring at her. He must have been in her eyes almost as broad as he was tall. Then he moved slowly around the wall towards our gate slowly repositioning his automatic rifle in his arms.

This was really creepy thought March.

'Bloody hell', she muttered, wondering what a Serb was doing there and of course thinking the worst. Completely tongue-tied she froze until, leaning over the wall, he uttered very slowly in English:

'Cup-a-tea, cup-a-coffee?' making the mime of drinking from a cup.

'Of course' said March relieved no end.

'Come in and sit down', in her best English accent.

'F*****g hell,' exclaimed the soldier, who was obviously British.

'The first person I come across on this bloody island is English!!'

'They will never believe me back at base when I tell them!'

March ushered him into the garden and onto our terrace and called me. Having served in the regular army I quizzed him on what he was doing here. It turned out that he was on an initiative exercise where he and several of his comrades were being dropped onto various islands to fend for themselves until picked up later.

I quickly pointed out to him that, due to the R&R training at the local hotel, and the army not wishing to upset the locals, the island was a no-go area for uniforms and weapons.

He was amazed at this because nobody in his unit seemed to know this ruling or that British soldiers were here. Probably not surprising as he turned out to be from the RAF Regiment.

I felt that it was better if I handed him over to the officer in charge at the hotel where he could stay until arrangements were made to pick him up. Having warned them at the hotel I smuggled him and his rifle into our car and into the hotel, where I later learned that he had an enjoyable time playing pool and watching satellite TV!

Later that evening we heard a helicopter. We peered out from our terrace to see it when it suddenly appeared flying low with the side door opened and "our soldier friend" and his chums leaning out to wave to us. He would no doubt dine out on his story for some time.

*

Chatting to Robi and Erika one evening on our terrace, Robi announced:" I get new car".

"Wonderful " I exclaimed.

"Well done well done" said March.

We were pleased for both of them as their old Citroen car was over 20 years old and almost falling apart. If it wasn't for the fact that Erika's father was a good mechanic it probably would have fallen apart or exploded.

"Business doing vell and I get good price for new Citroen in Split", said Robi.

Knowing from previous conversations that Erika didn't drive and that when Robi had on several occasions tried to teach her, they had almost come to blows, I made a suggestion.

"Why don't you hang on to your old car for a while

and I will teach Erika to drive on it". (not wanting to risk ours or their new one)

This met with universal approval.

"You werry brave" said Robi.

"Are you sure?" said Erika nervously taking a slug of red wine.

"Yes, we will start tomorrow!" I exclaimed; the red wine no doubt giving me Dutch courage.

The next day in the afternoon I duly went to collect Erika who was very nervous, and the car. I thought that I had better familiarise myself with the beast and duly climbed into the driver's seat.

"I will just drive along the Punta", I said noticing that Robi and Erika were both grinning impishly.

Having fiddled around with the controls I put it into gear. The clutch was really strong and difficult to release slowly except with great strain on the leg, nevertheless I managed to move forward without too much of a jerk; the other gears being not too bad to handle, but still a bit like driving an armoured car (a bit like the armoured "one-ton pigs" in Northern Ireland)

Then I tried the brakes.

I was a good thing that I was going quite slowly because at first nothing happened!

It was only when I started to pump the breaks furiously that I got a reaction. The steering wheel was also very stiff and very hard to control after being used to power stearing.

More than a little apprehensive now and wishing I had not suggested this venture I drove back and settled Erika in the driving seat. As she had driven the car before on her abortive attempts previously I did not have to start from scratch.

"Just put it into gear and we will motor up and down the Punta", I said calmly, not wishing to go anywhere the village.

Fortunately there were places at each end of the Punta for Erika to turn so we motored back and forth with only March, Robi and Lieka as spectators (most residents were weekenders so we were saved from cheering crowds).

In spite of the cars decrepitity and eccentricity Erika did quite well but I was glad that we kept to about 20 mph. We did this for about an hour during which she also had reversing practice at each end of the Punta.

We then adjourned to our terrace for a well earned glass of wine.

"Mr Mike werry calm at my driving", said Erika.

"Vait till you go tru willage", said Robi with an evil grin.

The next early evening Erika and I set off for the willage but instead of going along the harbour, which was filling me with dread, we went on the upper road past the church and up onto the road to Selca, bi-passing the willage. Whilst putting off the inevitable drive around the harbour, the road was steep uphill with numerous tight bends. Erika took to the task with great bravado, and although visibly nervous kept uttering girlish chuckles; not that this did anything for my sanity!

A couple of miles up the hill I spotted the entrance to a quarry with plenty of turning room.

"Ok Erika, turn in here", I said with anticipation of brief respite.

"Vill do", she exclaimed and turned perfectly in a complete circle.

"Vell done " I said imitating March.

" Right," I said. " We will now go downhill the same route, slowly, as the brakes are not too good".

Was this an understatement I thought, or my last words!

Erica set off and controlled the car well, pumping the breaks continually, and after some hairy tight turns at what seemed increasing speed we arrived at the last straight to the Punta above the willage. We arrived back to the obvious relief of Robi and March who were peering anxiously on our terrace.

After a few days of this route, which we extended further towards Selca, I decided that Erika was able to tackle the road through the willage around the harbour wall.

This could be a simple task or much more difficult, even for an experienced driver, if the harbour was full of strollers, people buying fish from the boats or veg from the veg lorries. Erica was not the slightest bit nervous and set off with great bravado to show-off to the willage her driving skills.

It seemed as though everyone knew that we were coming as people were leaning out of doorways and windows waving to us. What was alarming was that Erika was waving back with gay abandon, whilst the car drove perilously along the edge of the harbour wall.

"Erika, watch the wall!" I said calmly.

"Erika, the wall", a little more concern in my voice, followed by a lunge at the wheel to correct a swerve towards the sea, whilst Erika acknowledged the crowds.

Nevertheless, in spite of this hairy drive Erika had done very well after only a couple of weeks driving. We were all well pleased and celebrated over a glass or two of wine.

The lessons continued for a week or so and Erika grew in confidence and competence, even making Robi to remark: "You teach her werry vell you know, I test her on road today."

We decided that with a couple of professional lessons she should easily pass her test.

*

March had been a keen gardener and was determined to make our garden by the sea really lovely. The problem was the complete lack of garden centres. But she persevered in spite of everyone saying:

"No good for garden near to sea and Bura!" and "You will never grow plants there".

Erika had various plants and flowers around her terraces but they always seemed so sick.

"Do you ever water your plants?" enquired March one day.

"Sometimes", said Erika. "When I remember".

"You must water every evening in this heat ", said March.

But she understood perhaps why Erica was a reluctant waterer. It was only about 10 years before that the Island had no water supply, which now is piped across the sea. The locals had to collect water from their roofs into lined storage tanks below ground. Hopefully the water collected over the Winter and early Spring would last through the hot dry summer; water was therefore a very precious commodity and could not be used for plants and flowers. Erika did have though a very good little vegetable garden which thrived quite well.

On our trips away we brought plants back and March was particularly brazen in taking cuttings of plants she liked in other peoples gardens. I told Erika about this and she said:

"That good. Stealing plants, we say in Croatia, brings good luck!"

Gradually over 4 years March had a very pretty and colourful garden. I had done the labouring, which was my only attribute as far as gardening is concerned. I had also brought wheelbarrows full of flat heavy stones from the beach and built a false well, as a feature.

The garden was looking so good that on Sundays when the wives and children took strolls around the willage and out to the Punta, whilst their husbands played cards, they peered over our wall to admire the garden.

We eventually brought a TV, which had sound so we could enjoy the English programmes, which were numerous. One of these amazingly was Alan Titchmarsh in Gardener's World, with subtitles in Croatian. March was well pleased and also pleased but amused to hear from Erika that all the women in the willage loved Alan and his programme and would not miss it every Wednesday evening. We went to the Chelsea Flower Show the following year and attempted to tell Alan all about this but we could see he was more than busy. He would no doubt be amused that he had such a following in such an out of the way place. Strange that I come from the same place as Alan, Ilkley in Yorkshire, and that he has green fingers and I am quite the opposite; fortunately March more than makes up for that.

*

We were watching the television one day about Pula and Opatija on the Istrian peninsula; the area looked really lovely. We decided that we didn't explore enough and that now the motorway north to Zagreb and Rijeka was open the trip up there should be much easier.

We duly set off up the motorway which was really quiet like many French ones and took only 3 hours to Rijeka from Split, and a little bit further to Opatija on the coast. We were really impressed with the place; it was smart with a lovely seafront and very smart looking hotels. Most the hotels had been the seaside houses of the aristocracy of the Austro-Hungarian Empire and were regency in style. We found a lovely hotel right on the seafront with a charming room and ventured out to seek our evening meal. The seafront was a mixture of little market stalls, small cafes, bars and restaurants, so plenty to see.

"What is that lovely smell", asked March.

"I think I recognise it", I said, but could not put a name to it. And then I passed under the branch of a large tree.

"Bay tree!" I exclaimed. March agreed.

But the trees were enormous, and probably planted when the Austro-Hungarian Empire was in its heyday; there were so many of them too, which was why the perfume was so pronounced.

The other tree, which was in great profusion was the Wisteria. Indeed one restaurant with a large terrace had a complete canopy of Wisteria; it too must have been very old. We dined well that evening and enjoyed a stroll along the waterfront before turning in.

We spent 2 nights there exploring the town and along the coast; the peninsula is quite beautiful though in the height of the season in July and August is very crowded we were told, not only with Croatians but with hoards of Italians.

It was a lovely break, which enabled us to see another part of Croatia.

*

Things were beginning to happen in the village. We were getting more new people. Some Germans bought a house on the harbour and shortly after a young English couple bought only a few doors from them.

Henk, the American finished his house and he and his wife became regular visitors at weekends and holidays. Just along the Punta from them an Austrian family built a new, quite large house; though the style of architecture came in for some criticism from some locals.

Another American bought in the village; he was a brain surgeon, who offered to teach free of charge in one of the Split hospitals.

Also and quite dramatically we heard that the army were leaving. Apparently they could not agree the terms of the next lease so were moving the R&R centre to somewhere else.

The hotel would then go on the market. Many people would be sorry to see the army go because of the business they brought, but others said that Povlja needed the hotel to improve tourism as there were only a limited amount of holiday apartments.

We were impressed with the small boats with outboards that Simon had to rent so we decided to venture out along the coast. We had a boat in Jersey so we were old sea hands. Simon told us about a restaurant along the coast that was only accessible by sea and only about an hour away.

We pootled along the coast and explored the many inlets some with some very attractive properties with moorings and jetties. Then we sighted the restaurant. We saw the many yachts and powerboats moored there first with the restaurant nestling in behind. A goat was roasting on a spit and the lovely smells of grilled fish filled our nostrils as we hauled our little boat onto the shingle beach. It was pretty busy but we found a table and had an excellent lunch washed down with Dalmatian red wine. The restaurant was smart and well run by very friendly people.

As we left we also noticed another small rather scruffy restaurant about 100 yards along the bay. A small tourboat, probably from the mainland was moored there and its passengers were tucking into their lunch and wine; it must have been good as they were bursting into song!

This place became a regular haunt for us both for lunch and dinner and occasionally Simon and Susy would come too.

*

Apart from that life drifted on as normal. We kept up our routine of working on the house and garden or artwork in the mornings, a walk to the shop before midday, a drink in one of the bars to 'people watch' and relaxing and swimming in the afternoons.(relaxing was more like having a siesta!). We spent about 5 months there every year; splitting the time between Spring/early Summer and late Summer/Autumn. Giving the hot Summer months a miss as it really was too hot for us but not necessarily for others.

With this routine, our close friends and the lovely region of Dalmatia we had truly found paradise.

DRIVING LESSONS WITH ERIKA!

Epilogue

Our happy existence of spending half the year in Dalmatia and the other half in France and travelling was shattered one day when we were in France. We received an SMS from Erika saying simply: "My Robi just died".

We rapidly packed a few things and piled into our car and set off for Povlja, hoping to get there for Robi's funeral and to help console Erika. Sadly our car broke down in Italy near to Trieste and it took two days to repair so we missed the funeral. We were taken by Erika, who was very brave about Robi's death, to the family plot in the lovely cemetery on the top of the hill above the village, and paid our respects to our dear friend Robi.

After 4 years since Robi had had a malignant melanoma removed, and we all thought it had been a success, he developed frequent headaches. Erika had begun to ask us for paracetemol when she had run out and we expressed our concern; Erika eventually persuading Robi to see the doctor. He was found to have a tumour on the brain and had to go into hospital to have it removed. Again he seemed to be recovering well and was always cheerful and jolly. He continued to have treatment, in Split and Zagreb, and also went to specialist in Vienna; arranged by friends.

It was therefore with complete surprise and shock that we received Erika's SMS.

Erika had a double blow when her mother died 2 years later. She is bravely continuing with their little business based in their garage. Like us I'm sure she feels Robi's powerful personality around the Punta. We miss his booming laugh and the: "Hey neighbours!," called over the garden wall.

*

There have been other changes. The British Army have gone but the hotel sadly remains empty; the price no doubt too high for any investors the village needs to develop tourism and create jobs.

I must say I miss seeing those fit young soldiers, sailing, mountain biking, windsurfing, diving and so on; it was just like being back in the army for a while. I'm sure the bars will also miss the income.

Following the completion of the motorway from Zagreb to Split, the motorway is now advancing down to Dubrovnik, but I would always prefer the drive on the winding road along the coast. So travel is becoming easier and resorts much more accessible, including more and cheaper flights to Split.

We also have bigger and faster ferries on the Split to

Supetar run; only 45 minutes as opposed to over an hour on the Vladimir Nazor in the early days.

On the Ancona to Split run we miss the Marco Polo and Dubrovnik, which are now cruise liners.

There are now some more 'supermarkets' on the island in both Bol and Supetar. I say supermarkets but they are really large shops. Nevertheless, they are substantially bigger than the little village shops. They have more choice but I still prefer the squeezing down the narrow isles in our local one. I did however find a bottle of Worcester Sauce in one supermarket!

*

Life in the 'willage' goes on much the same. It is still the beautiful place we found years ago. Sadly, we miss Erika's pizzas but there is still good food to be had in the various restaurants.

Simon and Susy have had a little girl. Simon has also given up being the harbourmaster and hiring out his scooters and boats; they have moved to live and work near to Split on the mainland. Simon as ever is making really superb and innovative furniture; he is really an excellent carpenter and cabinet maker.

Most of all Povlja, to us, seems much emptier without our dear friend Robi.